"Whitespace is soul grace. Bonnie Gray ushers weary women into the real possibility."

—**Ann Voskamp**, author of the *New York Times* bestseller *One Thousand Gifts*

"Women need this message. If you want to hear Jesus speak more tenderly to your soul than ever before, this is the book for you. I love Bonnie's honest and unassuming voice. I will be recommending this message to many friends."

—**Lysa TerKeurst**, *New York Times* bestselling author and president of Proverbs 31 Ministries

"If you've ever been hurt and needed healing, if you've ever been afraid and needed courage, if you've ever been weary and needed room to breathe, then Bonnie Gray is the guide you've been looking for as you journey with Jesus to a new place of peace and freedom in your life."

—**Holley Gerth**, bestselling author of *You're Already Amazing*

"Bonnie's story captured me from the first chapter—she is an immensely powerful writer with a gift for taking her reader on a journey of experience. I felt like she was giving me permission to seek real, honest answers about my own walk through depression. Her story about loss, life, and love is worth its telling, and I'm glad Bonnie has told it."

—**Tsh Oxenreider**, author of *Notes from a Blue Bike: The Art of Living Intentionally in a Chaotic World*

"Bonnie's courage, heart, and determination to share her struggle are inspiring to me. To look back, gather pieces of what seemed unredeemable, and truly surrender them to the Lord is one of the hardest and most God-honoring things we can do in this life, and she does it beautifully. I would encourage you to read her words and allow them to sink into the places you've considered hopeless in your own life. By the grace of God, I hope you are able to emerge with the same tenacity, hope, and perspective as Bonnie has."

—**Angie Smith**, bestselling author of *Chasing God*
and *What Women Fear*

"Bonnie's story is a moving example of what God can do with our toughest struggles if we give him access to our hearts and minds. It also provides insightful exercises that will help you with whatever you are struggling with."

—**Stephen Arterburn**, bestselling author,
host of *New Life Live*, and founder of Women of Faith

"I just adore Bonnie's heart and her vulnerability as she allows us into her pain-filled, hope-filled story. Her willingness to open wide in order to help and encourage her sisters to find rest and spiritual 'whitespace' is brave and beautiful. If you've been looking for rest and you could use some practical ideas for finding spiritual whitespace, this book is for you."

—**Sarah Mae**, author of *Desperate: Hope for the Mom
Who Needs to Breathe*

finding
spiritual
whitespace

AWAKENING YOUR SOUL TO REST

BONNIE GRAY

Revell

a division of Baker Publishing Group
Grand Rapids, Michigan

Published by Revell
a division of Baker Publishing Group
P.O. Box 6287, Grand Rapids, MI 49516-6287
www.revellbooks.com

Printed in the United States of America

Library of Congress Cataloging-in-Publication Data is on file at the Library of Congress, Washington, DC.

ISBN 978-0-8007-2179-4 (pbk.)

Unless otherwise indicated, Scripture quotations are from the New American Standard Bible®, copyright © 1960, 1962, 1963, 1968, 1971, 1972, 1973, 1975, 1977, 1995 by The Lockman Foundation. Used by permission.

Scripture quotations labeled ESV are from The Holy Bible, English Standard Version® (ESV®), copyright © 2001 by Crossway, a publishing ministry of Good News Publishers. Used by permission. All rights reserved. ESV Text Edition: 2007

Scripture quotations labeled GNT are from the Good News Translation—Second Edition. Copyright © 1992 by American Bible Society. Used by permission.

Scripture quotations labeled Message are from *The Message* by Eugene H. Peterson, copyright © 1993, 1994, 1995, 2000, 2001, 2002. Used by permission of NavPress Publishing Group. All rights reserved.

Scripture quotations labeled NIV are from the Holy Bible, New International Version®. NIV®. Copyright © 1973, 1978, 1984, 2011 by Biblica, Inc.™ Used by permission of Zondervan. All rights reserved worldwide. www.zondervan.com

Scripture quotations labeled NIV 1984 are from the Holy Bible, New International Version®. NIV®. Copyright © 1973, 1978, 1984 by Biblica, Inc.™ Used by permission of Zondervan. All rights reserved worldwide. www.zondervan.com

Scripture quotations labeled NLT are from the *Holy Bible*, New Living Translation, copyright © 1996, 2004, 2007 by Tyndale House Foundation. Used by permission of Tyndale House Publishers, Inc., Carol Stream, Illinois 60188. All rights reserved.

Scripture quotations labeled NLT 1996 are from the *Holy Bible*, New Living Translation, copyright © 1996 by Tyndale House Foundation. Used by permission of Tyndale House Publishers, Inc., Carol Stream, Illinois 60188. All rights reserved.

Emphasis in Scripture quotations has been added by the author.

To protect the privacy of those who are part of the author's story, some details and names have been changed.

The author is represented by MacGregor Literary, Inc.

14 15 16 17 18 19 20   7 6 5 4 3 2 1

To Eric—
this book is a testament
to what happens when a man loves a woman.

And to Josh and Caleb—
because Mommy loves you.

contents

foreword

Somewhere along the way, we stopped valuing the idea of rest. We lost sight of the fact that it's a critical part of creativity. It's a critical part of our health and it's a critical part of our faith. As my own life keeps getting busier, I keep returning to Isaiah 30:15, which says, "In repentance and rest is your salvation, in quietness and trust is your strength, but you would have none of it" (NIV).

The repent part of that verse we get. We put that on signs and scream it from the rafters. We preach a thousand sermons on repentance for every one we preach about rest. And then our lives burn out, our pastors burn out, our families burn out—and we wonder why. We fight the idea of Sabbath as if it's lazy. Why do you think hundreds of thousands of vacation days go unused each year in corporate America? We live in a culture that brags and boasts about being busy. Into that reality steps Bonnie with a new idea.

Whitespace is an important concept and Bonnie has captured it perfectly. If you're tired of being tired, read this book. If you're exhausted with being exhausted, read this book. If you feel too busy to read this book, then that's probably the best sign of all that you need it.

Jon Acuff, *New York Times*
bestselling author of *Stuff Christians Like*

preface

The stories I'm about to tell were uncovered as memories tumbling out of my heart, the way a baby pushes out of the womb. It is a messy journey—a soul coming alive—tearing apart muscle and sinew of the past while trying to heal and put the pieces back together again.

Memories aren't always exact recollections of what was done or said. But they enable us to store and process what's happened to us.

There is a mystery to how the journey through sadness and loss can leave echoes of words on our hearts like the clap of birds taking flight over a canyon. But there is a greater mystery I'm finding in that chasm of whitespace left behind in the silence: God's whispers to rest.

This might not be the book I would write years from now, after straightening all the words and figuring it all out. If I wrote from the end looking back, you might think my journey to rest walked easy and wide. But that wouldn't be honest. Because it has traveled broken and narrow.

So I offer these pages more as a journal of intimate conversations between confidante and friend.

My prayer is that you will hear God whispering in your heart—to take the same journey. To allow your story and your voice to emerge from deep within. And to awaken your soul to rest.

introduction

My throat feels tight. Thick. I swallow hard.

I am doing one of the hardest things I've ever done in my life.

I am writing. To you. About why I've been away. About why I haven't written. But I must. There is no other choice—if I want to be free.

I must write, even though I am afraid. Even if I don't know where all these words will lead. Because Jesus is telling me I must trust him. With the truth of why I've been away.

The last time I tried to write this manuscript was one year ago.

You'd think writing a book on finding your spiritual whitespaces—places to enjoy soul rest with God—would be a beautiful experience, free from trauma and stress.

You'd think, in the same way spring gently blows cherry blossoms from stem to the water of a nearby stream, my thoughts would return to places of goodness, peace, and serenity—while living in the moment—as I wrote to you about the creative life of spiritual rest.

Doesn't an author get to live the topic she is writing, in order to tell its story to you?

That's what I thought. Until I started writing.

As I pushed into the heart of the manuscript, I was suddenly taken captive to places in my soul I had never been. I had just finished the first ten chapters. Everything seemed to align according to God's will and purposes for me.

To write.

To have a voice.

To be free.

And then it happened.

Trauma.

Trauma

The month leading up had been a nightmarish marathon of battling winter illnesses. Pneumonia and a nasty virus named strep collided with my boys, three-year-old Caleb and six-year-old Josh, for weeks. Sick little boys don't sleep well, spelling sleep deprivation for me. My husband, Eric, caught the flu and I ended up flat on my back with strep throat too. I was completely exhausted and utterly behind on my manuscript.

To get me back on track, Eric surprised me by booking a cottage at a local retreat center for some uninterrupted time away. I packed my bags and drove up into the mountains along Bear Creek Road. Nestled in thick foliage and the sound of dark night crickets, my heart surged with hope.

As I grabbed myself some tea in the cafeteria, I overheard other guests sigh with disappointment. We were caught in the heavy drizzle of a winter storm. But I was euphoric. A rainy weekend in a cozy cabin, typing next to a window with a view? A writer could ask for nothing more. I was golden.

Back in my room, I began unpacking, spreading papers across the floor in the layout of each chapter. I knelt to pray. I asked God to prepare his words for me. I asked the Holy Spirit to speak into

14

my heart for the work ahead. I thanked him for the beauty of his presence in my life. I spent the remainder of the afternoon revisiting passages of Scripture and journaling prayers to God.

It was the perfect way to begin my writing retreat. It would be time for dinner soon. As I gathered my coat, slipping my hands into gloves, I had no inkling of what was waiting ahead as I closed the door behind me.

Nothing could have prepared me for what I was about to experience. I have hiked in storms, rain soaking down into my socks, lightning and thunder crackling at every side.

Yet in less than ten minutes of walking up a muddy hillside, I was about to fall into the most terrifying, traumatic trek in my forty-one years of life.

Something Very Wrong

My heart started racing. Then it started pounding. My chest tightened. My throat started narrowing. The sky turned white and my entire world became oversaturated with light.

I couldn't see. I started feeling dizzy. Sick. Then nauseated. I wouldn't have been so alarmed if I hadn't started gasping. For air. Choking.

Oh my God! What's happening?

I fell to the ground.

I. Can't. Breathe.

I choked my way through the next dizzying minutes. How many passed, I don't know. I picked myself up, dazed and confused. I somehow brought myself to the dining hall and took spoonfuls of bean soup and bites of bread, sitting in the corner, shaken and cold.

That night, as I struggled with sleep in the dark, my body became flooded with feverish chills. Hot flashes.

I must be stricken with some weird, awful sickness. I thought.

The next day, after writing another chapter, walking on that same path, it happened. Again.

Something must be very wrong.

A Dangerous Endeavor

I returned home to see the doctor, but my tests came up normal.

Every night, for the next three months, I would fall fast asleep and then suddenly my throat would constrict and I would start choking. Hot flashes would fire through my body, sending my heart palpitating like crazy and my chest heaving as I struggled to recover my breath.

It took months of torturous insomnia, fear, and confusion, stumbling down rabbit trails and misdiagnoses, until I understood what I was experiencing. I went through a revolving door of doctors, counselors, and pastors—until I finally found an expert who understood the cause of my suffering.

I don't have cancer.

My faith isn't broken.

There isn't a hidden sin unconfessed.

You won't believe it. I didn't believe it.

Apparently, writing can be a dangerous endeavor. Writing this book on rest and peace opened up trauma from my childhood. What I experienced on that dirt path last winter was a panic attack—a symptom of *post-traumatic stress disorder.*

Yes. Me, the girl who has never been afraid of anything, is recovering from childhood trauma.

PTSD.

The Girl Who Wasn't Afraid

PTSD—me? Suffering from post-traumatic stress? It definitely didn't make any sense at all. *Hello, God. This is me, you're talking about. You know—the "Faith Barista" blogger—the one who has always trusted and loved you?*

Something else must be wrong, because with you, I've never been afraid of anything.

I'm the girl who

grew up first generation American-Chinese and put herself through college,

enjoys inductive Bible study as a hobby,

snowboarded double-black diamond runs,

loves people, snorts when she laughs, and regularly enjoys coffee with pastries.

How can this girl have PTSD?

Childhood trauma? C'mon. We're talking about stuff that occurred decades ago. Why would it surface as trauma now?

Apparently, trauma can be frozen in time. A person, an event, stress, or a change—even a dream or a hope—can unravel that trauma. This is what happened to me as I stepped into writing the belly of my book.

You see, there was an incident. Actually, more than one. People who hurt me in my past recently attempted to place themselves back in my today. And all the sadness I've swallowed, the losses I've dismissed, and the memories I've turned into stories suddenly ignited into live events up on that mountain.

Apparently, this girl does have trauma. Deep inside, I am, it turns out, very much afraid. A part of me—the wounded part—that stems from my childhood has surfaced.

A Search

As I stumbled into trauma, my world fell into a chasm of anxiety, panic attacks, and a continuous flow of broken sleep. Even though I was not conscious in the least about what bothered me, tides of emotional tears and empty feelings of fear and helplessness would overtake me. My thoughts became muddled with worries, big and small.

How was I going to finish a manuscript about rest with my life like this? A total and complete, utter mess. I couldn't even breathe right, much less write a single word about anything beautiful, serene, or restful.

Like a child discarded on one end of town, I felt dropped off in the middle of no man's land. I had nothing to offer to anyone. So I began my descent into the desert of stress and anxiety.

Like a wayward nomad, *I embarked on a desperate search for spiritual whitespace*—rest for my soul—in desolate places, in a land I had never wandered through.

Journeying Together

In the coming pages, I will tell you where this journey for whitespace has brought me. To be honest, I don't want to tell you about any of it. Because I don't want anyone to see the memories I'd wrapped so tightly to my chest for four decades that I'd forgotten they were even there.

Because it's rather embarrassing. You would think that a woman my age, a wife loved by her soul-mate hubby, a mom of two beautiful boys, a high-tech professional who has managed a career leading product teams, who has traveled halfway across the world as a missionary to help others find Jesus, would certainly know how to rest.

You would think someone who has trained others to study the Bible and launched ministries of friendship and faith would know better than to allow herself to spiral into a place of uncontrollable anxiety, especially at a point in life when a childhood dream to write a book was coming true.

If there was ever a time to write about the goodness of God and paint you beautiful pictures and tell you the top ten ways to find rest, it would be now.

But I don't have such easy words to offer to you.

I only have whispers, etched in pain. *And I speak them with hope and encouragement, to assure you that no matter what is in the past, we can walk forward on this journey of the soul. We can find the whitespaces inside us to rest together with Jesus.*

New Places of Rest

I step out to share my story with you because it is in these unexpected places of brokenness I'm hearing Jesus speak more tenderly—and I feel his hand fold into mine more gently—to lead me deeper into new places of rest. I would've never chosen to write to you about finding rest from these broken places. But this is where he's taken me to travel, and maybe this is why our paths have crossed here between these pages.

Because maybe Jesus wants us to know there is no place we can find ourselves where his presence cannot reach us. Because he is right here.

> If I make my bed in the depths, you are there. . . .
>   if I settle on the far side of the sea,
> even there your hand will guide me. (Ps. 139:8–10 NIV)

Here in the coming pages are the questions about rest I have asked and the answers as I found them.

Will you share your journey with me? Dare to bring all that moves your soul, breaks your heart, and whispers beauty to you?

Let's swap our stories and try to remember what it is that makes us dream and stirs us to write, shed tears, sing poetry, or miss the quiet on a cool autumn morning.

Bring it all and let's discover what the rest we crave from Jesus in our season of life looks like.

Rest, Jesus is whispering to you and to me.

Come.
   Let me be with you.
   As is.

Pull Up a Chair

It's time to restore our souls—to care for what's tender, what's broken, and what's fragile. As we do, like leaves turning crimson and golden, falling fresh onto the ground at dusk in the fall, we will discover what is beautiful: *who we truly are when our souls rest with Jesus and Jesus is at rest in us.*

So pull up a chair and stay awhile.

Let's meet with each other, chapter by chapter. Open a page in your journal and let's uncover pieces of your story as I unravel mine with you. Allow your thoughts to flow from your heart through your pen. Because maybe for you—as they have been for me—words are more than just ink on paper. They are soul prints of God's voice—carrying the unique timbre of heaven-on-earth that only you can speak.

I would love your company, because you are not making this personal journey alone. I'll be sitting down, walking through this book for the first time too.

You see, I've never openly talked about any of this. This is new for me. And because it is so, I need faith friends for this journey into the *spiritual whitespaces.*

Spiritual Whitespace

Whitespace. It's the space on a page left unmarked. Untouched. Whitespace makes art beautiful.

Whitespace is an important concept taken from the world of art and design. Whitespace is not blank—it breathes beauty and gives the eye a place to rest.

Without it, clutter takes over the art.

Our souls are canvases too, longing for quiet and beauty.

Just as beautiful art needs whitespace, we need whitespace: spiritual whitespace. *Our souls need rest.* To find balance and beauty.

Spiritual whitespace makes room—room in our hearts for a deeper, more intimate relationship with God, room in our lives for rest, room in our souls for rejuvenation.

This hunger for beauty, for *space for the soul to breathe*, resides within each of us.

My story is really every woman's story. Because every woman has felt burned out and tired. Every woman longs to dream, to feed her soul and rest. Everyone longs to move beyond coping and surviving.

Yet we often put ourselves to the side, numbing the stillness *by doing rather than by becoming vulnerable and real.*

To the artist, whitespace is paramount. It's a term used in visual arts to convey a very important element of design. It enables objects in a composition to exist at all, and it breathes beauty.

God is the Artist and Architect of the soul. He doesn't use up every single possible space on the canvas. When God looked at what he was holding—after placing his lips and breathing into the dust—he saw something come alive.

Something he never, ever made before.

It's what God sees, looking into your heart and mine today.

He is making something beautiful out of you.

A Beautiful Journey

God uses spiritual whitespace the same way an artist uses whitespace to imbue artwork with an indelible *aesthetic quality*—whether it be a painting, the still of a photograph, or a well architected home.

God uses whitespace in our lives to *reawaken our souls* with rest.

When we make room for spiritual whitespace, we step into the beautiful journey of letting go to discover what's really worth holding on to. To slow. To savor a moment. To enjoy a conversation. And renew an intimacy.

Let's uncover our stories. As we do, let's find the spiritual whitespaces in our souls and in our schedules to hear Jesus speak more tenderly than we've ever heard him before. Because the kind of beauty I am discovering—the creative act of spiritual rest—is found in places of brokenness.

When we step into whitespace, we are no longer holding on to our old ways of coping, managing, and doing. We are only holding on to Jesus.

He's there. Even though I don't want to go there.

In the whitespaces.

Our soul awakens.

To rest.

With him.

PART 1

a soul's beginning

In artwork, the use of whitespace
is not merely "blank" space.
It is an important element of design.
It enables objects in a
composition to exist at all,
and it breathes beauty.

1

desolate places

Off Script

All great and precious things are lonely.

John Steinbeck

I was a little girl, standing in the middle of the broken driveway sloping down into the busy street. I can still see the cracks splitting the cement into an odd-shaped honeycomb, crawling like varicose veins marring the ground beneath my feet.

I stood there, heart pounding in my ears, hot tears flooding my eyes. I cried with my mouth open, stuck in a silent howl unable to make its way out of my body. I knew I had to stop before I could turn around, walk up the steps, open the screen door, and go back into the house.

There was no one to comfort me. No one to tell me why he wouldn't be coming back. There was no one to hold me after my Daddy left. Not that day. Not that night. Nor any year after that.

And that is how I learned to take care of me.

Surviving

I am very good at surviving. I am an expert at figuring out how to do things right and do them well. I am not afraid of working hard, swallowing whatever might get me down, and pushing through.

I am a good thinker.

What I'm trying to say is I don't want to be that little girl, frozen in the driveway.

Needy.

Lost.

Confused.

So, I manage. I cope and I please.

I can do capable: set goals, check lists, and construct new plans. But deep inside, where no one can see, where I seldom go myself, I feel restless.

Unsettled. Disconnected.

My heart feels lonely.

I don't really see it as loneliness. Most of the time, I don't know what is wrong. So I tell myself nothing is wrong.

That I'm fine.

But I'm really not.

Because, you see, I feel numb.

Feeling Numb

I find myself there whenever I'm stressed. I step into another space of being that is separated from my heart. On the outside, I'm doing everything I'm supposed to be doing. Being with others and getting things done.

I wait until the numb feeling passes somehow.

When I was younger, I'd occupy this space of numbness by keeping busy, being extra social, or finding well-meaning, pur-poseful activities. But as I grew older, I found myself heading in

26

the opposite direction more frequently and for longer stretches of time: withdrawing. Being alone by myself, mostly.

Some days, after working hard all day, I was simply exhausted. I'd ease the numbness by passing time, staying up late "chain reading," watching television, surfing the net, or whatever it took to distract me from feeling.

But since walking into PTSD, my old ways of coping aren't working. Stress, worry, and anxiety have wrapped around me like a cut-out landscape painted around my waking days and sleepless nights.

Life has gone on pause deep inside me, where my heart spins restless.

I'm stuck.

Even though on the outside you'd never know. Because I step through the paces in everyday life and rise to the challenges of the daily grind.

But the truth is, I'm not free inside.

What I need—and what I don't have—is soul rest.

It took writing a book to wake my heart up and ignite my soul again.

Journey Off Script

If you ask me how I'm finding soul rest, it hasn't come the way I once learned. I haven't been able to spend alone time with God the way I used to as a little girl. Then, I'd set aside time to sit at my desk, open my Bible, take out my notebook, underline it with the headings—who, what, when, where, and why—and start diving in. When I prepared Bible studies as a ministry leader, I'd exegete passages of Scripture and come up with closing application questions.

No, I haven't been able to find rest for my soul in ways tried and true in the past. I can't even fall asleep, much less breathe freely, without a heavy feeling clamped around my chest, against a pounding heart. I can't even focus, much less memorize Scripture or pray like they taught us in Sunday school: praise, confession, thanksgiving, and supplication.

No, my journey of faith has gone off script—into my soul's whitespaces.

I no longer have the luxury of writing about spiritual rest behind the safety of studies, numbers, anecdotes, and experts' advice. I've never felt so desperate. For a lot of this journey, I have felt

guilty, unable to shake off my anxieties,

ashamed, tossing through insomnia-filled nights,

fearful of how others would judge me, and

trapped because I didn't know what to do.

My greatest fear was failing to find the freedom I believed came from walking with Jesus. It seemed that fear was coming true, as I found my heart and body gripped by panic and anxiety.

I never would have guessed in a thousand years my journey to rest would be paved with so much anguish. But the journey of the soul is one that Jesus is deeply and intimately familiar with.

I know this because Jesus has been living this journey with me. You see, Jesus has been meeting with me in the desolate places.

Desolate Places

Desolate places.

They're the last places on earth you'd look to find soulful rest. These were the places within me I ran from, hard and fast, the places where stress and anxiety overtake us. They rob us of our moments, abduct us from where we are. But surprisingly they are locations for whitespace.

Desolation is where Jesus went to meet with God. It's where Jesus chose to retreat. It isn't where we'd expect the Son of God to do his quiet time. It's the last place we'd think someone so connected to God the Father would go.

Yet Jesus sought out desolate places. When crowds pressed in around him for healing, Jesus was in touch with his needy soul. He withdrew.

Words written by those closest to Jesus give us a glimpse into his private world. Luke, a physician whose writing voice is punctuated by accuracy and specificity, tells us:

> But Jesus often *withdrew* to *lonely* [*desolate*] *places* and prayed. (Luke 5:16 NIV)

The Wilderness

I often drive to the mountains when I'm feeling lonely. I like to go in the morning when the sun hangs low, restless as it climbs out from behind the horizon. The ground is still soft, hidden under the frost of a winter's night. The hills lay bare, except for tree limbs stretching out like the arms of a child sleeping, tousled out from under her grandma's quilt.

I wonder what it'd be like to see Jesus walking up ahead, all by himself, quiet and slow. Would he walk like me, looking down at the ground, or would he look up into the distance, feeling the dirt stir as he paces through the morning air?

Eremos. It's the Greek word for *lonely.*

It means wilderness: *desolate*, solitary, lonely, uninhabited.

Deserted by others.

Deprived of the aid and protection of others, especially of friends, acquaintances, and kindred.[1]

The wilderness. Where I'm exposed, unsure, and undecided. Where I am stressed and anxious. No one to help and so very much alone.

This is where Jesus found me.

And this is the place from which I'm writing to you today.

Making Room

Enjoying time with God and finding soul rest isn't a matter of self-discipline, of trying harder or setting your clock to wake up fifteen minutes earlier. If it was a matter of simply willing yourself to do quiet time, I know you would have done it. You always have.

The journey of faith has brought you to a different place now. When your heart is troubled, your body weary, or your mind consumed with dilemmas and uncertainty, your soul is longing for something more than checking another box off a list.

Jesus may have led you to a place like the one I am standing in right now, hungering for rest. We've never traveled this far, this deep into our spiritual journey. Your soul wants to wake up, so it can rest.

He's calling us to find a new place of rest that goes beyond our ability to create it.

We can't make it happen.

In the same way the wind blows the first cherry blossoms from their stems in spring, Jesus wants to come into our hearts and release us to rest.

To be free again.

To feel.

To want.

To need.

And to be loved.

This is what I call making room for spiritual whitespace.

Spiritual Whitespace

In art, whitespace is often referred to as "negative space." It's the space on the page absent of marks or images. We might consider the space as "blank," but to the artist, whitespace holds beauty. *It is the key element of design that gives balance to a composition, transforming a cluttered collection of objects into an aesthetic expression of what we do see.*

Whitespace is anything but nothing. It is as important as the content being presented. When it is used, whitespace makes art come alive, injecting atmosphere and emotional depth, and creating movement in images that might otherwise appear static, disconnected, or flat. It is the *breathing room* the viewer needs in order to *experience* what's being presented and *find meaning* in it, whether it's a painting or a photograph.

Whitespace signifies space for a story.

It makes me wonder: Where are the whitespaces in my life?

So much of my stress has been driven by fear of empty spaces. I've skimmed over the deeper questions of desire and loss and made a life pretending they weren't there.

I did it to focus on the present rather than deal with the past. I thought that was a good thing, because this kept me strong. But the parts of me that once felt alive and free have slowly receded.

My soul isn't designed to be cluttered. It longs for space to taste beauty. To breathe. It's always wanted what God intended for me.

My soul was designed for spiritual rest: spiritual whitespace.

An Awakening

Making room for spiritual whitespace takes us on a journey to awaken our hearts to God again.

To investigate. To ask ourselves: Where is the attraction that once drew me into the safety, pleasure, and freedom of being with Jesus? And how can I find those places—those whitespaces in me—again?

Making room for whitespace means taking the journey to confide in Jesus the way we would if he were standing right here in front of us.

31

When we make room for spiritual whitespace, we create space in our hearts,

a blank space for Jesus to write on,

a white canvas for him to paint onto,

an intimate silence he can speak into,

a cool, dark night sky to light a song or lyric within,

an open field for him to walk through,

an intimate café corner for him to whisper into, and

an empty seat in the window of your soul, so he can lean in and wrap his arms around you as you both watch lightning crawl across the sky.

Finding your whitespace is daring to discover the places in your heart that are virgin, tender, soft, untraveled, wounded, or broken—so Jesus can make those places yours and his.

He is whispering—

I am here.
In between the cracks, where you've left yourself
standing there.
In the whitespaces.
Needing rest.
I'm still here with you. As is.

It's not easy following Jesus into the whitespaces of the soul. I have wallpapered over many things, believing faith enabled me to move past them. But there comes a time when it takes more faith to fall apart with Jesus than to stay strong enough to stop it from happening.

The time came for me to go beyond wallpapered memories, because Jesus walks the desolate places. And this is where my journey to find God and soul rest began.

Pull Up a Chair—Share

Picture Jesus withdrawing often to lonely places. What thoughts or feelings does this image stir in you?

Where are you on the journey to find rest—surviving, numbing, or awakening?

A Whitespace Prompt—Try This

Sometimes, we carry preconceived notions about connecting with Jesus. Trying to figure out how to spend time with God may be the last thing on our minds when we are stressed. But Jesus can enter into whatever space we find ourselves. As is.

Read through this list and notice which image reflects your heart's desire for whitespace most closely today.

a blank page

a white canvas

a quiet silence

a cool, dark night

an open field

an intimate corner of a café

an empty seat in front of a window

. . . [add your personal image]

What attracts you to this image? Notice how these images release you from the burden of creating rest with Jesus—opening your heart to experience rest with him. Rest is not something we engineer, but something we invite.

A Soul Conversation—Confide in Him

Tell Jesus how you are feeling right now in this moment. Lost, numb, tired, frustrated, or angry? Maybe your feelings are more subtle—content yet unsettled? Talk to Jesus now, friend to friend. Imagine him slipping away from everyone and everything else just to be alone with you right now.

2

wallpapered memories

Following Jesus

> Nothing is ever really lost to us as long as we
> remember it.
>
> L. M. Montgomery

I finally started sleeping at night a few weeks ago.

Not every night. Maybe one day out of the week. Then, two.
That strung into three.

It started happening randomly.

There was no formula. I'd been doing the same things, feeling
the same way, battling the same anxieties. But for some reason,
the nights I've been able to fall asleep—and stay asleep—started
emerging every few days or so.

I still have to take a light sleep medication. Ambien. It's the price
of admission, to have a chance of falling asleep. And I can't stay
asleep too long. Maybe five hours on a good night. But it is still

1000 percent better than what it was, which has been insomnia for weeks that stretched into months.

If I had been able to sleep at all, it had been broken. Two to three hour spurts, interrupted by hot flashes. Anxious thoughts. Panic attacks. And on the nights void of panic attacks, I'd just lie there helplessly as the night poured out into the dawn, tired and dark as molasses, even though I was so exhausted my eye sockets would ache and my bones throbbed with pain.

Sleep eluded me. This became my life for one year.

Wallpapered Memories

I certainly wouldn't have guessed sleep could return out of the blue. So out of context.

I had been working through one particularly traumatic memory in my life with my therapist, Dr. P.

This was a deep and painful chapter in my life.

I was seventeen.

As I've wrestled with these memories, it's made me incredibly heartbroken to relive them in the Technicolor-heightened sensory overload that comes with a nervous system amplified by post-traumatic stress.

And I've felt so very lonely and overwhelmed by grief.

Dr. P tells me this isn't me "now" who is drowned out by these intense feelings of numbness and excruciating aloneness. It is seventeen-year-old me, who has been frozen and sealed off by wall-papered memories. It's the seventeen-year-old me who has lived many lifetimes worth of aloneness and fear since she was four years old.

For the First Time

I haven't been able to even get out of bed most days. Even when I drag myself out to take a walk in the morning and enjoy intimate time in prayer with Jesus, I find myself going back to bed as a place of comfort.

Until it's time to pick up my kids from school.

Then I seem to come alive for them. I play with them. I go to Target, drive to Costco, buy my groceries, help with homework, cook, read Caleb stories in preschool voices and listen to Josh demo the features of his latest spaceship Legos.

After they're tucked into bed and the dishes are washed, I take my bath. I'll spend some quiet time sipping tea, reading, or listening to soothing music and reflecting on Scripture I'd read earlier in the morning.

And I go back to bed.

To brave the night once again.

Except this time, and for more than a few nights thereafter, things were different.

For the first time in a year, I've been able to continuously sleep without panic attacks choking me awake every two-three hours.

I was excited to tell Dr. P this one morning. Maybe I was finally touching the surface after tunneling through so much trauma. Maybe my body was beginning its release through the memories that have been reignited.

It Is Now Time

Dr. P was happy for me. He told me this was a big step in my recovery.

We proceeded with our therapy session, to process the remaining roots of the traumatic memory we've been working through. As I begin to gather my things at the end of the session, blowing my nose, and draining the last sips of tea, Dr. P says it is time for me to consider the next step.

"What?" I ask.

"It's important," Dr. P prefaces. "I want you to think about . . . reconnecting with your father."

The dad I last saw when I was seven years old? I don't think so.

"Just think about it. Talk to Jesus. See what he says," he prompts.

Just when I started sleeping again, he wants me to do *what*? Open a can of worms to more emotional drama?

No way. Nothing to think about there. At least that's what I thought.

Your Full Voice

My therapist, Dr. P, is a world-leading expert in treating PTSD. He tells me panic attacks typically strike the strong. CEOs, pastors, managers, stay-at-home moms, writers, and everyone in-between. You don't need to have fought in a war in Afghanistan or Iraq to suffer from PTSD, and it's not limited to victims of physical or sexual abuse either.

The impacts of emotional and verbal abuse are equal in damage and trauma.

PTSD often surfaces in people in their thirties and forties—when major life changes are occurring. The stresses we've hidden deep inside finally emerge when we can no longer bolt down what we fear most: *our wounded selves.*

God knows I've prayed about everything, forgiven as needed, and "buried them at the cross of Jesus." What's in the past belongs in the past, right? *Forget what's behind and strive toward Christ ahead.* That's been my motto.

That's the thing. I believed my faith buried my hurt in the past, but I was using faith to hide from the past. God hasn't forgotten. He's saying to me now—

Bonnie, it is time for you to heal.
I don't just want you when you are strong.

I love you when you are broken.
And I don't find it shameful that you are wounded.
You want to only speak in that voice that feels safe and
good.
But I want you to speak in your full voice.
Where I am your only safety.
Where I am your only good.

It's hard to stop and investigate. Why are we stressed? Who wants to feel wounded? Not me. I was like the agoraphobic who avoids going to the grocery store because that's where she had her last panic attack. Like the man who won't cross a street because that's where he was hit by a drunk driver.

Me, I've avoided touching my childhood with a ten-foot pole. I kept waiting for my symptoms to go away. I wouldn't want anyone to think I'm broken. *I want to present my good and unwounded self.*

But Dr. P says that day would never come if I didn't "cross the street," even if I am afraid.

I didn't have a choice if I wanted to be free. Because Jesus was calling me to put my faith in him in a new way—by investigating the wounded me. And I was terrified.

Immovable Parts

The week before my next therapy session, my mind kept returning to a scene in the Bible where a man was lying next to the pools in Bethesda.[1]

He was an invalid. He could not move.

He could only lie there day after day, next to the pools that were rumored to grant him healing if he made it in first, when the waters were stirred. But, somehow, he could never touch those waters in time. He was trapped. For thirty-eight years.

Out of all the people who piled around the pools hoping for a miracle—lame, blind, handicapped and suffering—Jesus saw this one man. Jesus asked him if he wanted to be well. Then Jesus asked him *to pick up his mat*, the one he had been lying on for thirty-eight years.

Pick up my mat. *What is the mat you want me to pick up, Jesus? What realities have I accepted living with for decades that have become immovable parts of my identity?*

Like the paralytic man chained to his place by the pool, how have I adopted ways of coping, managing life, relating, and surviving that are keeping me from healing my soul?

Follow Downstream

It dawned on me.

Bonnie. Your panic attacks aren't going away.

What's worked for me since I was a child—staying strong, reading more Scripture, praying more fervently, exerting more self-discipline, applying greater optimism—isn't going to solve this problem.

Jesus has been whispering one phrase into my heart—

Follow the current downstream.

I've rowed my boat upstream for so long, I didn't know if I could stop.[2]

Are you afraid where it will lead?
 You can be afraid with me.
 Follow me downstream.
 Investigate.

Like the sun faintly lit behind fog rolling through coastal skyline, these words drew me to seek a therapist to help me. Here I am now, one year later, asking: Jesus, are you asking me to do what I've vowed to never do?

Are you asking me to look for my father, thirty-five years after the day he cried into my shoulders and drove off, leaving me with his tear-choked words, "Say bye-bye to Daddy. Daddy isn't coming back anymore."

> Hear, O LORD, when I cry with my voice,
> And be gracious to me and answer me.
> When You said, "Seek My face," my heart said to You,
> "Your face, O LORD, I shall seek."
> Do not hide Your face from me . . .
> Do not abandon me nor forsake me . . .
> *For my father and my mother have forsaken me,*
> *But the LORD will take me up.* (Ps. 27:7–10)

Pull Up a Chair—Share

How is Jesus placing the word "follow" on your heart today?

How is Jesus prompting you to pick up your "mat"?

A Whitespace Prompt—Try This

Get curious about yourself. If you were to stop fighting to stay strong—to stop rowing upstream—and allowed God to take your heart downstream, where would it lead?

Jot a Downstream Dare list. Validate the journey of faith God has you on. Explore what lies downstream.

Yeses. What would you say yes to—if you could investigate things you've been avoiding or afraid to explore? What is a next step?

Nos. What would you say no to—if you could—in order to stop rowing? These could be expectations, rules, people, or places that stress your heart.

A Soul Conversation—Confide in Him

What is keeping you from speaking in your "full voice"?

3

the toy store

Receiving

I float around this world like a fallen leaf,
Grant me now the solace of your sympathy.

Ryan Kingsmith

I don't know what it is about rain.

But there's something about the way it falls. The way it smells when it first hits the pavement, as it begins to dot the blacktop into a dark, wet chalkboard. Everything looks clean and new. The ground looks so smooth, I could glide on top if I broke into a run and slid right onto puddles filling up invisible dents.

I wish it had been raining the day I stood in the driveway of our house early one morning years ago. The tires on the olive-green Nova my Daddy rolled up against the side of the porch were gray and worn. The roof of the car was black, peeling, the way skin does when you scratch your arm against the side of the bed, trying to fish your book out from dust bunnies.

I didn't want to be afraid.

It was supposed to be simple. Just a visit. My parents had divorced. I didn't know it at the time, but it was going to be our last visit together.

I was seven years old.

I Knew Better

I was supposed to climb into the back, onto cracking vinyl seats, into the car with the peeling rooftop. It smelled like dirty ashtrays in there. But I didn't say anything.

I kept quiet as my little sister with chubby wrists and cherub-rose cheeks toddled in to sit beside me. I felt small and awkward, shoulders hunched, as my father turned and smiled a little too widely, his eyes sad and lonely. But I didn't know what to do, because my momma said nothing about this visit. Other than telling us not to take anything from him.

As we rode across town, over the train tracks, past the metal factories and smokestacks of the old Del Monte cannery in Sunnyvale, everything looked eerily silent. It was Saturday morning, everyone still in bed. The streets rolled by empty, as I wondered where we were heading.

I still remember how big the KB Toy Store looked as my father tried to hold my hand walking through the parking lot. Even though my little sister couldn't read, she knew where we were. She was excited, her little feet hurrying ahead.

But I knew better.

Nothing ever came simple for me.

Rest for my soul feels the same. True rest is not so simple.

The Innermost You

As a theological truth, I know I can rest. The book of Hebrews tells me Jesus is my high priest, brokering for my peace with his body and his blood. From an intellectual perspective, I know I need rest. We're humans, not robots. Lots of studies show how important it is to my well-being.

Prior to experiencing PTSD, I would've told you I was pretty good at being restful. I drink tea; love hiking, friends, and pastry joints; and sip coffee. As an introvert, I like to read, and taking a bath is a ritual at the end of the day.

But deep inside, where God says he desires truth—in my innermost being—I am a stranger to soul rest. When I'm most conflicted between what I want and what I ought to do, I'm soaked in deep need within my innermost being, standing in the *whitespaces of my soul.*

The Psalmist David sensed this need for deep, soulful rest. He confesses the secret we all carry. He has no idea how he can find this rest. He asks God to find him in the whitespaces.

> You desire truth in the innermost being,
> And in the hidden part You will make me know wisdom.
>   (Ps. 51:6)

In my innermost being—in the hidden places inside—I've always worked so hard to rest. I've experienced peaceful moments. Yet I can't say I've held on to it long enough to make rest my soul's everyday home.

Deep, soulful rest is the harder path. It touches *the innermost you.* When we enjoy whitespace, we whisper, *God, I want the innermost me to be with you.*

This is not easy because I often prefer safety over intimacy.

Suspicious

I've had to make my own places of rest to shield myself from the world by planning well, solving problems, and pleasing others. It's the kind of rest that is easy to check off, but it locks up my heart.

Even trusting God became a test of my resolve. Rest became a battle to run away from the things that break me—instead of allowing the brokenness to bring me to him. All this running, it's exhausting.

Because whenever I stop and face the silence, I have to face the truth.

I am suspicious of a restful life.

I don't believe it can really, truly be mine. Just like the toy my father wanted to buy me that day at the toy store, I knew it would never be mine.

Frozen

I was standing in the toy store aisle. Frozen.

My father wanted to buy me a toy. But I wasn't supposed to take anything from him.

So I told him I didn't want anything.

I'm okay. But I wasn't.

It's funny how the most terrible memories of the past can smooth out over the years to simply become a story you tell yourself. It's a familiar scene that unrolls every now and then. What he said. What I said. How the floor of the store shimmered under the gloss of florescent lights. How happy my sister was, picking toys off the shelf like she won the lottery.

I never realized all the emotions I felt at that moment could freeze inside. I am learning that some of the stories I've merely viewed as childhood memories are still *live events*—behind the steel trapdoor of my heart.

I thought I had moved past them. By growing up. By depending on God—in the sincerity of my heart—to move myself further away from the little girl in me, who was afraid, who didn't know what to do.

Deep inside, that little girl is still there. Deep where I've never held any regard for fear, confusion, or neediness, there is a part of me who is very much alive: *the girl in me who carries my father's wounds.*

You can't see that part of me by looking on the outside. I certainly didn't, until recently.

The Right Thing

I am starting to remember—the look in my father's eyes.

"Daddy can't be with you anymore. . . ." His voice stumbles. His head drops. I notice the side part in his hair, as he crouches low. I start to feel very nervous. It doesn't feel right somehow, him so sad, so up close.

"Daddy just . . . wants . . . to. . . ." He starts choking back tears. Swallows hard. Looks straight into my eyes. I see pain.

He struggles to finish his sentence. Tries again. "Daddy . . . just . . . wants to . . . buy you a toy."

I can't tell you exactly what was running through my mind. But I know how I feel right then and there. Thickness fills my little body from the top of my head down, dropping down through the beating heart in my chest to the bottom of my feet.

I feel trapped. I don't know the right thing to do anymore.

What should I do? What will happen if I did one thing—or the other?

What will happen to him? What will happen to me?

The Wound

As I stood at the checkout register, with my father pulling out paper bills from the wad of cash in his pocket, I froze again, fearful what would happen after my ride home.

I didn't want him to pay for our new toys with his hard-earned cash. But, as he placed the plastic bag of toys into my hands and tried to reassure me, "It's gonna be okay. . . . It's gonna be okay," I knew it wasn't going to be okay at all.

That day I took the plastic bag was the day I began carrying invisible wounds that cut deep into my soul. I wanted so badly to

take in comfort I desperately longed for,

open my heart and tell him which toys I liked best,

cry into his shoulders and ask him, "Why can't you come back?"

Instead, I stood there motionless, trying to decide what to do and whom to please. As I did, something inside me started to crack and bleed.

A wounding took place in my heart so faintly, I didn't even know that it left me *split apart* that day. The part of me that wanted life to be simple—to love my father and to let him love me—separated from the part of me who knew better.

I lost a beautiful, fragile part of my soul that day: my ability to simply receive.

So, I taught myself that day: I do not need to receive to be happy. Avoiding pain and figuring out whom to please was more important.

These are the wounds I carried by taking that toy back home with me. Things didn't turn out okay that day. Even though I tried to do the right thing. Even though I tried to believe life could be simple in that moment again.

What's Rough and What's Jagged

It's easy to talk about the beauty of whitespace if you look at an empty canvas. I once stood in the San Francisco Museum of Modern Art, peering into three panels of white, mounted on a gigantic wall that reached high into a ceiling that echoed your breathing.

The artist titled it *White Painting*.[1] There was nothing else painted on it. Just a roller of white. Simple. Smooth.

That's what I've tried to do. Time and again. I take my roller of forget, try to wipe away anything and everything inside that hurts, that worries me and makes me sad. I smooth out frazzled fragments of memories so nothing disturbs my peace or breaks my faith.

But life doesn't work that way. We aren't empty canvases. We can't really smooth out what's rough, what's jagged in our souls. Even though we try.

Finding spiritual whitespace isn't about carving out an hour of time to escape the things that stress us.

It's the opposite. It's getting away from everything we do to distract ourselves from *all the hidden pieces*—in order to nurture our soul. It's getting away from the lie that spiritual rest is something we have to work hard at in order to get closer to God.

Spiritual whitespace moves us away from making spiritual rest an activity to please God, instead of enjoying his comfort and pleasure.

Spiritual rest is a journey of awakening our hearts to fully receive.

An Intimate Movement

Rest is an intimate movement to receive.

> Come, all you who are thirsty,
>   come to the waters;
> and you who have no money,
>   come, buy and eat!
> Come, buy wine and milk
>   without money and without cost.
> Why spend money on what is not bread,
>   and your labor on what does not satisfy?
> Listen carefully to Me, and eat what is good;
> And delight yourself in abundance.
>   (Isa. 55:1–2a NIV; v. 2b NASB)

These words read like a foreign language:

come . . . thirst . . .
buy . . . eat . . . without money . . .
wine . . . milk . . . delight . . . abundance . . .

It seems just too good to be true. Crazy talk.

Soul rest folded into these words feels so much more intimate than I've ever dared to believe. *What kind of rest is this? Can all this really be mine?*

My heart recognizes this questioning voice, because it has learned it is safer to hide than to stay open long enough to receive. Happiness is overrated. Why hold on to something if I might regret it? It might be taken away. It may not last.

The Gift I Lost

As I walk through this memory with Jesus, now grown up, I realize the gift I truly lost that day many years ago was *the gift to rest and receive.*

I know, Bonnie. Jesus whispers. *I know this wound.*

"What do you want me to do?" I ask him.

Come.
Let me.
Stay here.
With you.

"Please. Tell me what to do," I plead again. "I need to do s-o-m-e-t-h-i-n-g about this."

Tell me, Jesus prompts. *What is it that you need? What is it you desire? And why are you afraid to take it in?*

I don't want to stop and explore these questions. It's easier to not look inside for answers.

It's not so simple, taking the dare to receive. Because I didn't want that toy my daddy once tried to buy me in the store years ago. I didn't want it because I knew as soon as I got home, that gift wouldn't be something I could keep.

Pull Up a Chair—Share

Do you find it hard or easy to receive?

How is God taking you on a journey to rest and receive more deeply?

A Whitespace Prompt—Try This

Maybe, like me, you haven't been given permission and freedom to fully receive. Maybe, like me, you've been put in the disorienting position of *being split* between what you desire and what you fear. The journey to rest may begin with a prompt for your soul to speak with Jesus—without fear or judgment.

Delight. What feels comforting to you? List the things you like that bring your soul comfort. Uncover some whitespace by savoring one of these things this week, no matter how insignificant it feels.

Abundance. What do these words mean to you?

milk

wine

delight

How can you add a little more movement to receive for the *innermost you*?

51

A Soul Conversation—Confide in Him

God values truth in the *innermost you*. Share with him—what wounds have you lived through in your journey to receive?

4

cut up

The Harder Path

The human heart has hidden treasures,
In secret kept, in silence sealed.

Charlotte Brontë

Sometimes it's hard to know the difference between how you feel and where God wants you to go.

I've taught myself time and again to never trust my feelings but instead to trust in what my mind tells me is right. This way of thinking has helped me get through bad times and accomplish a lot in life. I've come to trust it, but I'm beginning to wonder if it's keeping me from enjoying the good times.

Not to say I haven't had good times. I've experienced amazing seasons of beauty, happiness, and contentment. But I'm talking about goodness deep in my heart, where I struggle with self-doubt, where I dream of living free to pursue my passions. It's where I struggle with feelings of unworthiness, even though I am grateful for everything God's done for me.

I am thankful God loves me, but I still feel I'm not quite good enough.

No Reason

I decided to tell Dr. P I wasn't going to look for my father.

There was no reason to do so. I haven't had a father since I was seven. What's the point? He never came back to see me. Not once. Not one letter or card.

I've often secretly wondered if my father had fallen ill. What if he had cancer? Maybe that's why he hadn't come see me all these years.

Around junior high or high school, a social worker helped us by insisting we get some sort of child support from our father. He started paying $100 a month.

$100 a month? What can $100 do? Is that all I'm worth to him? Why wouldn't he try to send me a little more, on my birthday maybe?

I knew he wasn't dead because the checks kept coming. I wanted to know more, but I couldn't ask.

Let's Talk about Why

I told Dr. P I didn't want to talk about my father. Maybe someday, after I write my book. *Hello, do you remember?* I thought. *I still have that book contract hanging over my head.*

"Let's just put this on the back burner," I said nicely. "I don't want to open this can of worms now. I'm beginning to finally, finally get some sleep."

"Well, let's talk about why you don't want to see him." That was Dr. P's response.

Arrrggh. Sometimes I wish Dr. P wasn't so good.

The interesting thing is, I've got this anxiety and panic attack "shock collar" on me, so if I don't follow through on the therapy I'll have physiological symptoms to deal with. I am logical. I want to get well. So I go along with this line of reasoning, if only to get him off my case.

"I just don't want to. Don't have any desire. Don't feel any need," I tell him.

"Think back to the last time you said these words about your father. What was happening?" Dr. P prompts.

I Didn't Want To

I close my eyes. And think.

The morning my father left, my mother asked me to come over to her. She sat in the living room with our family photo albums pulled out, stacked on top of each other.

She told me, "Come here."

She started opening up the photo albums, flipping through the plastic pages and pulling pictures out of pockets. The sound of film sticking to plastic tore through my pounding heart as memory upon memory was being ripped out.

"What are you doing?" I asked, sitting on my knees across from her.

"Start taking out pictures of him," she commanded. She shot me a look that told me I better not ask why. "I don't want any pictures of him in this house. Not one. I don't want to see his face anymore."

I don't know why exactly, but I didn't want to do it.

It made my stomach feel heavy and empty all at the same time, seeing the missing gaps in photo albums I'd flipped through so many times in the living room, lying on my tummy, swinging my legs barefoot in back of me.

I didn't want to take the pictures out.

I remember watching her cutting them up. Into tiny shreds.

Just Fine

She made sure the shears cut straight into the faces, until there was no recollection of the images that were once there. I held one last photo of my father, by the time we got to the end.

I paused, thinking, *Is there any way I could hide this one?*

My mother looked up at me. "What are you doing?"

"Do we have to cut all of them up? Can we keep just one? I'm not in this one. You're not in it either. It's just him."

"Why do you want to keep one?" she asked. A flicker of hope. I thought of a good reason, the only reason that surfaced in my confused heart.

"So I'll know what he looked like." I said it, just like that.

"Why do you want to remember what he looks like?" Her eyes narrowing into me, her voice sharp as the scissors in her hands. "Do you wanna go live with him?"

She got up and started marching to the mustard-yellow phone hanging on the kitchen wall. "That's what it is! You like him so much, why don't you go with him then. Don't live with me. Go pack your bags. I'll just call him now. And he can come get you!"

"No, Momma! No!" I screamed.

I bolted from where I sat, instantly flying into sobs, pleading for my life. She had thrown me out on the porch before and threatened to throw me away to the orphanage down the street when I was younger. I believed she'd do it.

It was there, when I was slumped over crying in hysterics, eyes hot from choking tears, my mother warned me, "Don't you ever talk about your father again. From this day forward, you don't have a father. With a loser like him, you don't need a father. Plenty of people grow up not having a father. It's just like being born with handicaps, without limbs. People grow up and do just fine without them."

Momma paused to make sure it all sunk in, before she laid in her final words of warning. "And don't you *ever* complain about not having a daddy. If you have any problems in life, it ain't gonna be because of me and it ain't gonna be because you have no father. It's gonna be because of you."

Right then and there, I straightened up. I stopped crying. It came clear as a bell.

I don't need a father. I don't have a father. I'm going to be just fine.

Separated

I realized, sitting there in the therapist's office, calm and strong, with my tears all of a sudden stopped, where my words originated from. I was still back there—standing seven-years tall in front of my momma—convincing myself nothing was wrong.

I was just fine. I didn't need any comfort. Nor any tenderness.

Then and now, I wanted to go on with the business of life and get back to a productive place: separated from my heart. This is how I've lived my life. Fine and functioning, but frozen.

And now Jesus softly whispers into my winter landscape, *Come out, Bonnie.*

Just as he called Lazarus out, wrapped up in shrouds of linen, Jesus is now asking me to emerge from where I've forgotten myself. Out of touch with my heart, I feel awkward.

Who wants to look all bandaged up, disheveled, and unmade?

Why can't I be sure before I follow my heart? I want to wait until I've figured it all out and put things back together again. But it seems there's no other way of finding my heart than to experience the truth of it leading me, with Jesus beside me.

What if this is all wrong? What if I'm just imagining all this?

A Part of Ourselves

Jesus is whispering—

It's okay.
This is how spring feels like to winter.
I haven't forgotten you.

The original English word for Lent is *spring*. As I walked the last two weeks of Lent into Easter, I sensed God turning my heart toward spring.

Jesus is prompting me to step out to rest in a new way with him. It's so much easier to take care of everyone, to tend to problems and everything else. It's easier to be strong and not need or feel.

We've been taught our feelings are not reliable, so we throw them to the wayside. *Trouble is, there is a part of ourselves we throw to the side too.* Sometimes the harder path to rest is following your heart and holding on to nothing but Jesus.

Let's not take the easier path. Let's take the harder path to rest, paved by new ways of faith. Let's take those feelings to Jesus and speak to him as friend to friend. Let's listen to Jesus speak to us in a different way—

in the voice of intimate confidante,

where he takes our tears and shows us where they lead,

so we can whisper all we've never dared to share.

This is the harder path of faith I'm learning. *Putting our hearts first—letting Jesus love us—is a new way of resting with him.*

The Way of the Heart

Lent is about denying myself the comfort of old ways—living out of my control and safety zones—to discover the truth of my heart with only one safety: Jesus holding me.

This is what I'm thinking when Dr. P prompts me to answer the next question.

"I want you to go back to the last time you were with your father." As I close my eyes, I'm wondering maybe . . . perhaps . . . if the way of the heart is where Jesus is waiting for me. He wants me to walk back into the past with him, so I can journey further than I've ever gone before.

This way of the heart led me to return to a long-forgotten screen door.

> For the LORD comforts his people
> and will have compassion on his afflicted ones. . . .
> "Can a mother forget the baby at her breast
> and have no compassion on the child she has borne?
> Though she may forget, I will not forget you!
> See, I have engraved you on the palms of my hands."
> (Isa. 49:13–16 NIV)

Pull Up a Chair—Share

When have you felt cut up?

How is Jesus whispering "spring" to you, prompting you to take a different path and rest with him?

A Whitespace Prompt—Try This

Are you facing a dilemma? Rather than drawing up a pros/cons sheet, which can separate you from your heart, picture yourself as a little girl. What would she choose and why?

A Soul Conversation—Confide in Him

Putting your heart first. When have you recently put your heart to the side? Share this with Jesus. What does he say?

whitespace is extravagance

Rest Is Choosing

In graphic design, the more

cluttered a layout is,

the more text and images crowd the print.

The purpose is no longer beauty.

It is commercialization.

Whitespace is *a choice*

to convey *quality* and artistic *value*.

5

the screen door

Space for Her

Let nothing disturb you. Nothing distress you.
While all things fade away, God is unchanging.

Prayer of St. Teresa

I didn't want to get out.

But Daddy swung the car door open.

He kept telling me, "It's okay. It's okay." But I didn't want to walk up to the porch. My legs drilled down into the ground like roots to a thicket of thorns at the bottom of concrete steps.

My Daddy put one hand on my back, pressing me forward, as he grabbed my little sister's hand in the other. He rapped on the screen door while I blinked and sucked my breath in.

As I held myself there for a million years, the door flew open.

There she stood. Over me.

Even behind the screen, I could see Momma clearly. Her ragged jawline, her teeth clenched and face flushed. Her chest heaving.

She took one look at me, at the plastic bag I was holding. I could see it in her eyes.

Red. Hot. Anger.

And I broke apart in a thousand pieces right then and there. I knew I shouldn't do what I did next, because it would make everything worse. But, I couldn't help it.

I started shaking. Tears began to erupt and my mouth pulled down into a trembling sob. I couldn't swallow them down. So I began to cry.

I Don't Want Her

I'm not sure what happened next, but I remember they started yelling at each other. My mother flew into a rage, stomping her feet and shooting her arms out as she stormed at my father.

"You!" My mother fired at me, shoving the screen door open. "*I told you* not to take anything from him!" I stood there like a dummy. "You like toys so much?" She snatched the toy from me and hurled it to the ground.

My little sister started howling. My mother took her toy too and threw it at my father. "I told you I don't want any of your stupid garbage in our house!"

My daddy tried to pick my sister up to console her, but my momma pulled her out of his hands. My daddy tried to yank the screen back open, except this time, my mother punched the door into his face.

I saw my father stumble backward, his glasses falling off his nose, his hair flying into a mess all over his face. My head started pounding and I saw my father crumble right before my eyes. He leaned into the beams of the porch, shaking his head, consoling himself with expletives.

Then my father quickly told me, "Go in, Bonnie. Go in." As he opened the screen door to let me in, my mother blocked my way.

"Let her in," my father said.

"Oh, you want to be the good guy?" Momma said. "Well, you take her then. . . . I don't want her. You can have her."

I don't want her. I remember those words.

Have you had these words thrown at you? Have you felt them smack against your heart, leaving an echo of pain across your soul? Whether it be a friendship, a job, good health, an opportunity, a community we tried to enter, a dream, a child we wanted, a man we've loved, or parents—aren't these the words we fear will fall into our ears?

These are the words I felt doomed to hear if I didn't become someone who deserved to be loved and cherished.

Nothing Special

Nothing special. Nobody would ever say it as bluntly as I heard it yelled into my little head that day. These are the inaudible echoes whispering at me to earn straight As, get my engineering degree, and land my first job out of college.

The whisper of *nothing special* sat next to me in my career even though I sat high on the organizational chart. Those words whisper to me just as loudly now, as I till the soil of my children's hearts as a stay-at-home mom, and in friendships that end up as one-way relationships. They hiss at me loudly, because I don't want to fail.

You are nothing special drove me to fall brokenhearted in the mission field as well. Because let me tell you, there are people who would love to determine your worth based on what you can do for them there too.

I've carried this uneasy suspicion I was nothing special and everyone would probably know it if I ever stopped doing and simply was plain old me.

There was no place for whitespace in the world for someone like me. There was always *the next thing* I needed to be or do for someone or for some higher purpose.

65

There was no place for whitespace where I could simply be. Because doing so meant settling for who I was. And that never seemed good enough.

Nothing special was the voice of the little girl in me. Waiting to be loved and seen. I've never stopped long enough to listen to her until Jesus led me back to that in-between place he knows oh so well.

That In-Between Place

"I don't want her." Those painful words lingered in the air.

I tried to hurl myself across the doorframe to get back into the house, but my mother pushed me back out. My daddy moved up behind me, shoving me back in. Before I knew it, I was thrown back and forth between them—volleyed across the screen door opening and shutting, arms flying, wild angry voices yelling. Like a metal pendulum ball colliding in Newton's cradle, I was launched in perpetual motion.

As I sat there in the therapist's office describing the scene with my eyes closed, Dr. P interjects. "Back it up. Play the scene in between the doorway again. Look into your mother's eyes and tell me what you see."

I rewind the scene and look into eyes of fire, a scowl emblazoned across her mouth. Then something seismic happened. Like a pistol shot in front of a sprinter cocked and ready, my body suddenly explodes into the scene. It's like that burst of pain that sears through your insides when you put on your headphones not realizing the volume is on maximum blast.

In that cacophony of scuffling back and forth, I hear a little girl's voice whimper and shriek. I'm frightened with white-hot panic because I recognize her voice.

It is mine.

In that instant, I was no longer the Bonnie who never knew pain.

Before I could take my next breath, a slap lands across my face. Even though I'm completely conscious that I'm sitting on a couch at the therapist's office, I feel my body falling. I see pieces of the sky spinning as I sail between choppy swirls of screen door slamming, arms pushing, and the weight of my head whiplashed sideways, back and forth. The swinging door flies out and smacks me hard against the side of my head.

I tumbled out onto the porch and my mom slams the door shut. Nobody's child.

"I feel . . . really . . . dizzy," I eek out to Dr. P. "I . . . can't . . . breathe."

I start choking in the session and a wave of nausea presses into my gut so hard my body tightens, lurching forward, ready to heave.

I don't know how long this went on, maybe only for a moment. But when I returned to that *in-between place where no one wanted me*, I was forever changed by the truth of what happened to me that day.

I Can't Take Her

As I stuff my receipt for that day's therapy session into my wallet, I tell Dr. P I can't do this again. "I don't need to revisit any more repressed memories. They're repressed for a reason."

"I don't think you can *not* process these memories," Dr. P offers sympathetically. "You've been too strong for too long. You're long overdue. You can't keep her sealed off in the past anymore."

"Yes, I can. I always have." I'm defiant.

"Well, she's been rejected already once in her lifetime. Do you want to reject her again?" Dr. P gently prods.

"Who are you talking about?" Wasn't Dr. P talking about my mom?

"*You*," Dr. P answers. "I'm talking about *you*."

Whitespace Is Extravagance

In graphic design, whitespace is a key element to the aesthetic quality of a composition. The more fine art a composition is, the more whitespace you'll find. The more commercial the piece, the more text and images you'll find crowded in. The purpose is no longer beauty. *It is commercialization.*

Designer Keith Robertson puts it this way:

> White space can make or break the effective transmission of image and text space. White space is extravagance.[1]

Whitespace is anything but nothing. Whitespace is a *choice* to convey quality and artistic value. Whitespace says we are someone special. It says we are fine art in God's eyes.

Whitespace keeps the message from being cluttered and draws attention to what's important. Am I trying to control the message my life is reflecting by filling it up—while avoiding the images I'd find if I stopped to rest?

Is my faith more like art or cluttered advertisement?

Whitespace is a beautiful principle applied to art hung on the wall or houses photographed for coffee-table books. But it's easier to perform—to improve ourselves—rather than rest when it comes to our own lives.

Because nurturing our souls is a dare to believe the outrageous: *I was created for beauty.* Because protecting the "negative space," the "empty space" in us says: *I am wanted. As is.*

What if our brokenness revealed more about God's love for us than our efforts to cover it up? Painting whitespace into our lives is extravagance.

Yet extravagance does not feel right on me, because whitespace brings me back to the little girl no one wanted.

To Be Known

Even now, as I finish this chapter, I'm struggling. I'm trying to type words onto the screen but only blank space stares back at me.

If you've ever experienced anxiety—the kind that wraps around your heart with the cloak of stress—you understand how it tethers you back.

It keeps you silent.

Keeps you in your home.

And on the hours or days you need to be with others, you end up retreating from being seen. Or heard.

You work hard. You get things done. But you might feel like I do, unsure if things can change.

Whether you can really be known.

This is soul wearying.

A Place for You

You may have been hurt, like I've been—*by words that wound you still*—that make you regret you shared.

Words that make you feel even smaller than how you're already feeling.

Words that make you feel pressured to get over what you can't get over.

Words that make you feel more alone, standing on the outside of *where you want to be*: belonging, loved, and understood.

At that moment, you and I chance upon a glimpse into our souls, into the little girls inside us who are broken, feeling cast off and lonely. It's hard for me to whisper to her, as I really long to:

I see you. And I won't put you to the side anymore.
Because Jesus is bringing you closer to me—
I'm learning to make a place for you in this world.

Jesus has a way of slipping in his love notes to reach that little girl in me. Just this morning, as I listened to piano music streaming from Pandora, the words he shared with his disciples those last hours floated their way to me.

Don't be troubled. You trust God, now trust in me. There are many rooms in my Father's home, and I am going *to prepare a place for you . . .* so that *you will always be with me where I am.* (John 14:1–3 NLT 1996)

A place for me. Just for me. With me. *Always.*

I've always read these words as words for the future, when I'll be able to look into the eyes of Jesus and finally lean into the sigh of his arms embracing me. But this morning as I heard them, I felt the still, quiet whisper of Jesus speaking to the little girl in me.

There is a place *here and now* that Jesus has been preparing for the little girl in me. That place is my heart, where Jesus has been doing deep, healing work—to accept her as she is. To let her know there is a place in this world for her.

Because Jesus understands her.

Because Jesus loves her. As is.

Make Some Space

His words to that little girl now, in this very moment, are—

You will always be with me where I am.
You will always have a place with me.
In you.

So even though we are all grown up and capable—carrying the load of daily chores, caring for others so they don't have to feel the strain we've had to endure—will we dare to ask ourselves:

Can I make some space for that little girl in me?
To begin a journey to walk out into the world?
To share her voice?

Even if she should be rejected—which you and I know she will be—we can remind her that Jesus loves her. And that, even so, we can try to find a friend. Maybe two.

Encourage her to believe—there is a place for her in this world.
Comfort her when she cries and doesn't believe.
Be patient.
Show her kindness.
Don't give up on her.
On that little girl in you. And in me.

Love's Imprint

Faith, after all, just can't possibly be journeyed alone, even if experience tells us we can do it ourselves.

We can learn to offer each other the kindness of Jesus and moments of safety. These small moments may be few, but they are enough, because love's imprint can never be erased. And it speaks to us through the words we share here.

This place in our hearts Jesus has made.

Just for us.

The real you. I'll be hearing these words for the first time as a little girl, as I make my way to the memory of a basement of an old Victorian. A long time ago.

> And this hope will not lead to disappointment. For we know how dearly God loves us, because he has given us the Holy Spirit to fill our hearts with his love. (Rom. 5:5 NLT)

Pull Up a Chair—Share

Have you ever felt caught in the in-between place: wanting to be yourself yet afraid to be loved and known?

Do you find it easy or difficult spending time and attention on yourself: feeding your soul, enjoying your artistic pursuits, or nurturing your body?

How can you walk the little girl in you out into the world?

A Whitespace Prompt—Try This

A letter from Jesus. Write a letter from Jesus to the little girl in you.

What does he want to say to her? What does he see that she needs?

Give yourself permission to write this letter. Allow God to love her through you.

A Soul Conversation—Confide in Him

Close your eyes and picture yourself as a little girl with Jesus.

How do you picture her, and what is she doing?

How does she feel? What does she want?

Express what's on your mind and heart to him. Tell it all to him. Look into his eyes. He is listening.

6

the basement

The Real You

Our scars make us know that our past was for real.

Jane Austen

I was just four. I know this because we were still living in San Francisco. We lived in an apartment in the basement, in Chinatown. In an old Victorian.

The apartment was always dark and the lights dim. In the living room, two rectangular windows streamed sunlight in. I could see the sidewalk from there, legs walking by, shoes pressing sticky in the rain, kicking up hems of raincoats and bellbottoms against the city's puddles. It's where I watched gray skies pelt water down against the windowpane.

In my mind's eye I remember standing in a dingy white kitchen where the spanking chopsticks were stored in the top drawer. My mother was angry. I had done something wrong and the palms of my hands felt the sting.

She grabbed my arm and yanked me out to the living room, to the media console next to the television, where the vinyl albums were stacked sideways on the bottom shelf. She pulled one out and shook it in my face. It was the record soundtrack from a movie and the album cover pictured a little girl looking frightened, in tears, clutching her arms tightly around her mother, who was being torn from her.

My mother told me if I wasn't good, I'd end up like that girl on the cover. "I don't have to take care of you, you know," she said matter-of-factly. "There's an orphanage down the street, where bad boys and girls get thrown away. . . . And I can throw you away there anytime!" *Did I want that?*

It's not clear what I said in return, but Dr. P tells me to look down at my feet in this memory. *What was I wearing and what did they look like?*

I didn't even know I could remember such a thing. But it turns out memories hold peripheral vision. Like a camera on the set of a movie, we can zoom in.

I look down and see my stubby toes. And they are tiny. And all of a sudden, I feel it. The hardwood floor—cold—under my feet. I'm suddenly shivering, because a chill has slipped over my body. I smell the musty San Francisco fog seeped into the walls. Mildewed, damp, and dusty. I hear the house creak as tenants walk upstairs.

I realize in a pit of panic I've returned. Back. *There.*

Abandoned

This was no longer a story I was narrating. Like a riptide curling around my ankle, this memory pulled me under, back to that cold, dark basement, one frightful day in San Francisco.

My heart started pounding in my head and my body shook un-controllably as an indescribable fear flooded my system. Tears like darts of fire poured out of me, as my little toes standing barefoot gripped the floor and my ears burned with terror.

It's funny how you remember the yelling. You can't hear the words. You only see the eyes. The scowl. And it's very loud. So loud the air around you feels like it's going to blow up.

She left me that way. Scared out of my skull. She grabbed her coat, slammed the door, and stormed out of the house. *Where did she go?* I cried.

I ran to grab a stool, pushing it up against the living room wall so I could peek out at the sidewalk through the window perched up high. There my little fingers gripped the windowsill as I stood tippy toe, desperately scanning the legs of people passing by, hoping to see my mother's emerge.

I don't know how many hours she was gone, but I thought she had left me forever. *I was abandoned.*

It felt like my mother would do this time and again. She'd eventually come back, with a bag of groceries. She would return acting like everything was just normal. And nothing was wrong. But each time she left, I always feared it would be the last.

I felt as Brennan Manning describes in his memoir *All Is Grace*:

> As I think back on my childhood, the word *shame* serves as an umbrella. It is the sense of being completely insufficient as a person, the nagging feeling that for some reason you're defective and unworthy.[1]

I looked for peace in unfettered serenity, but Jesus knew it was time for a deeper peace.

A Deeper Peace

Have you ever felt abandoned? Threatened to be thrown to the side emotionally? Have you, like me, tried to move on and forget about what happened—what we heard, saw, and felt—yet carrying the feeling of shame left by the journey?

There is a peace Jesus longs for us to taste, but it's not how we'd ever imagined it would come. You and I may have been running away from the basements in our lives, but Jesus is still back there, waiting there, to say to us—

I see you.
  I was there. I remember.
You are real.

Shalom

A deeper peace. It's what *shalom* really means. It's found in the beautiful original Hebrew language that gets lost in translation. *Shalom means wholeness. Real. Complete.*

> You keep him in perfect peace [shalom]
>   whose mind is stayed on you,
>   because he trusts in you. (Isa. 26:3 ESV)

Perfect peace from God isn't found by forgetting. Peace is ours if we dare to remember our pain and our sorrow, and experience our fears fully with Jesus. *Shalom peace from God is a putting back together.*

Shalom is the movement to recover pieces of ourselves that have been abandoned, a putting back together of what we've left behind, to find Jesus with us in our memories.

> O Lord,
> We have waited for You eagerly;
> Your name, even Your memory, is the desire of our souls.
>   (v. 8)

Healing. That's what Dr. P calls this journey through places of misery. How can anything so pitifully useless to me today as painful memories be any source of healing?

I'd been skeptical from the beginning. But as I left Dr. P's office that day, I would've never guessed that I would lie on my pillow and pass the night, for the very first time in months—free from panic attacks. *Somehow, reliving the past with Jesus was bringing me peace.*

Not an Eraser

The next night, the panic attacks returned. A new set of memories attached to the one in the basement surfaced. And so this cycle continued. Each time I processed a memory, a set of new flashbacks emerged. I get a reprieve the night of therapy, and the next day the chaos begins again.

Dr. P tells me I'm regaining more of my soul. But I feel so utterly broken.

I don't want any of this. I've been crying out to Jesus, calling for him to rescue me with peace that surpasses all understanding. *A miracle. Please. I know you can do it*, I pray.

Peace has not come to me this way. Not as an eraser. It's the opposite. Peace is only returning with each broken piece of my story I'm recovering. One memory at a time.

Peace is coming to me like sand dollars washing up en masse after a storm blows through. The clouds are still dark and the shore looks like the surface of the moon. Deserted. You step out onto the windswept beach and notice, one after another, sand dollars battered by the waves hiding in the sand.

You dig them up. *They are broken.* Instant peace is no longer a place of faith.

Shalom peace is now my new place of faith. My journey to find rest is now a journey toward wholeness. A putting back together that includes broken pieces.

The journey of rest is leading me to recover all of my soul. This peace makes no detours around reality.

You Are Real

Even as I sit in worship service on any given Sunday, a wave of anxiety can hit me. My heart starts pounding and my throat begins to constrict. I have to get up and leave. I can't sing. I have to sit outside on the patio.

The memories aren't stopping because Jesus is saying, *You are real.*

Like broken sand dollars that have escaped the storms of the past, memories are resurfacing. What happened at the screen door, the toy store, and more. I've been living under an *emotional amnesia* I thought was peace, but God is making my heart real with rest.

Free to Remember

The world may view our broken stories and tell us it's better to hide them. To forget the shame we carry, put on a smile, and disappear under the work we do, the people we please, and the frenetic activity of keeping busy.

Spiritual whitespace brings us to a different peace where we are real. Are you walking through a storm in your life, where you see parts of yourself from the past resurfacing? Are you afraid to move forward because it brings you back to where you've been hurt or insecure? There may be a challenge in your life—a change in health, a marriage that is shaking, a friend who has left you, a dream that is fading—that puts you back in dark, scary places.

Sometimes we can't escape the places we find ourselves. But we can turn to Someone who has faced the trap of darkness, even though he was the Prince of Peace.

Jesus lifts his cup to us. *Drink.* His eyes are full of pain. Our pain.

He offers us a plate of broken wafers. *Eat.* It's his body broken, crumpled on the cross, shaking uncontrollably from the pain.

Can't there be any other way? Jesus sputtered. With his heart doubled over, choking in agony in the Garden of Gethsemane, he didn't want brokenness either. Yet he chose to be wounded by it.

Jesus understands how conflicted we are.

Remember me, Jesus whispers. *Because I remember you. I was there back then, and I'm here with you today as you walk through those broken places.*

I am beginning to hear Jesus's words, even though I tremble to accept it: *I love you broken.*

Jesus is leading us to the operating room of grace, where the past isn't forgotten but remembered. *We are free to remember.* This is God's gift to you. And me.

God Does Not Forget

Being healed of the past can't be done by trying harder to live a good life. I've tried. *Please, God.* I'd whisper. *Deliver me.*

I didn't understand that remembering is a miracle of God's healing. God doesn't forget the basement. He doesn't forget the words, the abandonment, or the fear.

> Remember these things . . . for you are My servant;
> I have formed you, you are My servant,
> O Israel, *you will not be forgotten by Me.* (Isa. 44:21)

We can move on because God does not forget. We can accept the unacceptable because we aren't invisible. With every painful remembrance—the sounds, the smells, the fear tearing through your chest—our Abba Daddy saw everything and felt every stab of panic.

God is bringing us back into the past to give us a gift we've always wanted: the presence of a loving father. *Himself.*

When I see that my Abba Daddy has never forgotten me as a little girl, it gives me courage to discover who I am as his daughter today. I am free to be the authentic me.

Authentic You

Spiritual whitespace is a journey to discover the *authentic you*.

I'm just beginning to grow into the real me God's created. The shadow life I've lived is slowly giving way to the authentic me. It's changing how I spend my time and who I want to spend it with. I have stronger preferences now for what I want to do and what I don't want to do.

It's scary to feel so much. But I'm learning new things about myself. How I withdraw from joy, how I'd rather choose being functional than "waste" time on childlike interests.

Rest is taking away the veil, trusting God loves the authentic you.[2] This new world of whitespace can feel disorienting—doing things that yield no use to anyone other than being God's cherished daughter.

If you've ever found yourself in the middle of a dark storm—or you're standing in the calm after living through one—look down on the ground you're journeying through. Let's pick up the broken pieces the tide's brought in.

We can turn over shells that have been trampled on, flecks of white half buried in the sand. Because anyone who has ever stopped to pick up sand dollars after a storm will tell you—*bring a yellow beach pail*.

Among the ruin, we will find perfect, whole sand dollars. They're hidden on the shore, mixed in with the broken pieces.

We will collect them. You and I.

As I began to unearth the real me of long ago to find shalom peace, I had to confront a very important question: *Will I choose joy?*

It's not so simple, because I'd rather not think about an old pink outfit. But my soul could not continue awakening to rest unless I did so.

Pull Up a Chair—Share

Where are you on the journey of *shalom peace*—of being put back together?

How is God inviting you to discover more of the real you?

A Whitespace Prompt—Try This

Sand dollar reflections. What helps connect you to pieces of your past?

> Visit your hometown. Drive through the neighborhood with a friend.
>
> What is your earliest memory of being happy? Sad? Write it as a story.
>
> Take a picture of people, places, or things that reflect your early stories.
>
> What kind of music did you enjoy listening to as a child? Play some tonight.
>
> Do you have a favorite childhood dish or dessert? Cook and invite a friend over to enjoy.

A letter to your younger self. Think of yourself at an earlier time in your life, at an important milestone of the real you. What would you say to her now?

A Soul Conversation—Confide in Him

Where is your "basement"? Meet with Jesus through the pages of a journal entry. Consider confiding in him through a friend.

7

the pink outfit

Choosing Joy

The world breaks everyone, and afterward,
some are strong at the broken places.

Ernest Hemingway

I stood on the escalator next to him, one hand on the rail, as we
rose higher to the upper level. It felt so grand to be in such a fine
place: the children's department at The Emporium. It wasn't a
place where we usually bought our clothes, but today was different.

It was one of my father's first visits after the divorce. I was
excited because he said I could pick out whatever I wanted. I saw
manikins propped up like scarecrows on steel poles, posing with
pink purses and flowery skirts, sporting blond bob-cuts and auburn
ponytails. I walked around the racks of pretty clothes, a bit shy
touching what I usually could not buy.

My father shuffled beside me with his greased-up hair, baggy pants, and wiry legs moving in sync with my curiosity. He looked out of place among all the ruffles. He would pull out something random off the shelves and present it to me. *This is pretty . . . you like?* Then we'd move our search out to the next cluster of hangers.

Then I saw it.

Hanging up high, perched on a special display, was the most beautiful outfit I ever saw: a soft bubble-gum pink corduroy jacket with silver buckles and matching pants.

It was perfect. It's hard to explain, if you've always had nice clothes or if the thought that something was worn or mismatched never occurred to you. It looked amazing to me. Which one I should get—the jacket or the pants?

As I stood there on tippy-toes, reaching out to fish the outfit down for closer inspection, my father walked up next to me. He told me to stand still and held the outfit in front of me with one arm shot straight out, eyeing me like an old woman threading a needle.

"Turn around," he said, pressing the sleeves against my wrists. "It fits. Daddy will buy both for you."

As I stood there at the checkout register, watching my father pay, I couldn't believe it. *The whole outfit?*

My heart was bursting, full of something beautiful. New. All for me. I felt so happy hugging that big bag, walking down those fancy wax-polished floors, as my father held the door open.

Never in a thousand years would I have guessed I'd never even have the chance to wear that jacket and those pants out in broad daylight. They were thrown in the garbage later that night.

A Perfect Moment

We didn't have a garbage disposal back then. So my momma took whatever leftover gunk was found in the sink and dumped it on top of my outfit, with the tags still hanging off of it. I stood there in that gloomy kitchen in the dim yellow light and fading wallpaper. Devastated.

I don't have anything good anymore. It's gone.

I felt so lonely. Something I thought was perfect and mine was no longer any good.

I thought it fit perfectly when I tried it on in front of the mirror in the hallway. I could tell from my mother's eyes that this was the furthest thing from the truth.

"You look ridiculous," she spat.

Maybe this is when I first learned how completely lonely a feeling it is to hope for joy. Maybe that was the beginning of how I grew to believe living for moments of joy only meant leaving room for disappointment. This is why it is hard to talk about dreams if you've once had them come true only to have them smashed to pieces.

It's easy when you're young to believe dreams can come true. *But if you've ever truly had a perfect moment carry you to a place of belief*—whether it be a positive pregnancy test, a romance, friendship, a parent, your health, a career, a ministry, or maybe a lifelong passion, a home, or a new endeavor—and then had it taken away, *then you know what it feels like to see something perfect end up in the refuse of broken dreams and mismatched opportunities.*

You begin to wonder whether anything is worth delighting in again. *Is anything really worth enjoying if it can't last anyway?*

Perfectionism

This is why joy feels dangerous. Because for some of us, joy is connected to times in our lives where it was taken away or ruined, when a simple moment of happiness was decimated by a person, place, or thing. This is how I learned as a little girl to hope for safe things.

I didn't want to have my joy end up in the trash again. I wasn't trying to be a martyr, but I did not choose joy for the sake of having joy. I was happy without too much of it. I didn't *need* it.

Still, I couldn't bury the parts of my soul cracked by the shame of feeling ridiculous and ill-fitted. Feeling inadequate is a lonely feeling and I coped by becoming self-reliant, performing, and meeting other people's expectations for a very long time.

This way of life is called perfectionism. And I was good at it. I was well rewarded by people at work, friends, family, and even ministries for my ability to anticipate and do what people wanted.

There is an unintended side effect with perfectionism. It offers protection but your soul remains lonely. Loneliness is extremely exhausting. I slowly lost touch with the things that made me laugh, that moved my soul and made me love the quiet.

I was numb to delight. I stopped dreaming. I worked hard to gain comfort and security rather than joy, until Jesus caught me unguarded in a moment—

I was there, Bonnie. I stood beside you, as you cried.

As you looked into the garbage and saw something you loved being destroyed, I was there. And I'm here with you now.

I heard Jesus whisper these words into my heart one morning as I walked on a trail lined with thorns and thistles dried by the summer heat. I felt fearful writing this chapter, worried I had nothing to offer but depressing words of imperfection.

The Side of the Road

Then Jesus called to my mind a man who was battered.

Imperfect. Bruised. Ugly.

"Who is my neighbor?" a lawyer asked Jesus. He wanted Jesus to tell him the right thing to do. *Spell it out in black and white,* that's what he wanted. *Define the terms clearly so that there will be no more ambiguity.*

Instead, Jesus told him a story of a nobody on his way to Jericho. He didn't have a name. He was just a man, beaten, lying on the side of the road. Nobody stopped to give him any attention. He was just *damaged goods* to people who had places to go and important names to meet.

But, Jesus said, oil and wine were poured onto this man's wounds. Precious oil and wine splurged on wounds. I knew exactly why Jesus was telling me this story.

Joy. Joy is the oil and wine missing from my life.

Jesus understands the wounds where joy was demolished. Where something beautiful fades into the sidelines of our stories. Where we're only left with memories of what could have been.

I heard Jesus say to me as I felt those wounds surface—

Your wounds are not invisible. Your wounds have value to me.

Jesus reminded me this man was carried to a place of rest. His stay at the inn was paid for. Completely.

I will never run out of rest for you, Bonnie.
   No matter how much you need.
   No matter how long it takes.
   I will care for you.

Kindness. Compassion. This is the answer Jesus gives to the lawyer who was an expert at doing things right. It is rest Jesus longs to pour out onto the tattered parts of our souls.

Joy is the oil and the wine that heals our souls to a resting place.

The Joy-Wounded Stranger

Jesus shows us a new way of resting in the story of a wounded stranger on the side of the road. I've always read this story seeing the wounded stranger as someone else. Not anymore.

I know that wounded stranger has always been me.

It's the part of me I've neglected, a casualty stripped bare on the side of life's highway. That stranger is me, too wounded to step closer to joy. That joy-wounded me is a *time waster* to the Levite busy getting back to his temple duties. The joy-wounded me is an *unacceptable risk* to the priest, who doesn't dare touch anything lifeless.

I am both Levite and priest because I pass by the joy-wounded me. I'm exhausted by trying hard to be useful, so I'll never end up staring into a bag of garbage and feeling unloved and unknown—again.

Making room to awake our soul to enjoy whitespace, to explore delighting in things that make us laugh or smile, brings perfectionism to a place of acceptance and rest. Finding rest isn't about doing away with desire or eliminating the need to feel special. Finding rest isn't forgetting we ever had dreams.

At the end of the story, Jesus tells the lawyer to go and show "mercy." In Greek, the word is *eleos*.

Eleos is *kindness* and *compassion*.

In other words, Jesus is telling me to stop on the side of the road of my busy life and take care of the joy-wounded me. Jesus is telling me *to break away* from neglecting my soul. Joy is an act of faith—to offer kindness and compassion—to the joy-wounded stranger in you and me.

But, it is hard to give joy practical attention, isn't it? Choosing joy can feel like the most awkward and peace-threatening position to take. That's because we've survived long enough without making joy personal. We've never given ourselves the chance to look closer and explore what joy looks like for us.

Jesus is calling us to the Rx of spiritual whitespace: to expend the time, energy, and expense to pour joy on the wounded stranger in us. Just like he would do for me, if he were here in person.

Jesus is waiting. I stop so easily for others. *Will I stop long enough for me?*

The Rx of Joy

Choosing the Rx of joy in whitespace may not feel intuitive or right. When we engage in what brings us joy, we will feel vulnerable. We will want to retreat. We will say to ourselves:

"It won't last." Jesus whispers: *It doesn't have to. Look at the flowers in the field. How beautiful they are, yet I've made them to only last a few days* (Matt. 6:28–30).

"I feel guilty/selfish." Jesus replies: *Never will you be called forsaken. You are called my delight. Joy is meant for you* (Isa. 62:4; John 15:11).

"I feel stupid." Jesus stands by us: *I have chosen you. So do not fear, for I am with you; do not be dismayed. I will strengthen you and help you* (Isa. 41:9–10).

"It's too late." Jesus gathers us close: *Do not despise these small beginnings. You are big in my eyes* (Zech. 4:10).

"I will get hurt." His love can give us courage: *Place me like a seal over your heart, like a seal on your arm; for love is as strong as death* (Song of Songs 8:6).

"This is a waste of time." God assures: *You aren't a waste of time. There is no sunset, flower, or rainbow that does not reflect the time I spent making it come alive with color and feeling. You are no less* (Ps. 8:3–6).

That Pink Outfit

When we prioritize time for ourselves, to draw near things that bring a smile to our hearts, to enjoy pastimes that make us feel special, we are reaching for that "pink outfit." That pink outfit uniquely matches your personality, history, and makeup. The things that touch your heart.

We all have old pink outfits—the ones that were taken from us or destroyed. But God can help us recover the *courage to reach for a new pink outfit* today.

Each time we reach for joy, we take the step of faith to say, "This is mine. My Father in heaven knows what I like and I'm learning to discover it too."

This journey of joy is a recovery of the joy-wounded us. And Jesus is the one who can take our hand and guide us through this terrain. He can give us the rest of joy.

We can sample how joy feels for our souls. Joy is organic. It changes through different seasons. So let's give ourselves permission to try new things. See how they fit.

Investing in the Rx of joy in whitespace might look like we're off to the side, wasting time doing nothing. But if we look closer, we will see someone stepping out of eternity to make our hearts his every day, to care for you and me. That someone is Jesus, kind and gentle, never tiring, always longing to whisper in different ways—

You are worth it. You are loved. You are cherished.

How is this possible? I echoed back. If God loved me, he'd let me sleep. I wouldn't lie on my bed, night after night, with insomnia.

Pull Up a Chair—Share

When life gets hard, do you find yourself withdrawing from the care and attention your soul needs?

How is God calling you to stop on the side of life's busy highway, to nurture and awaken your soul to joy?

A Whitespace Prompt—Try This

Sample joy. Brainstorm a list that gives your soul joy. Resist the urge to evaluate.

People—

Places—

Things—

Interests—

Colors—

Foods—

Music—

A Soul Conversation—Confide in Him

What is your *old pink outfit*—the one that's been destroyed?

What would give you joy today? What is the *new pink outfit* you want the courage to reach for?

PART 3

whitespace is movement

Rest Is Freedom

A rest on a music sheet marks an interval
of silence, breathing a pause.
It allows music to resonate in
beautiful harmony.
In the art of photography, whitespace
is used to create *movement*,
evoking mood and emotion.

8

insomnia

Self-Care

You have made us for yourself, O Lord,
and our heart is restless until it rests in you.

St. Augustine

I'm trying to sleep. But I can't seem to stop thinking.

I know I shouldn't worry so much. So why am I still lying here in the dark awake? I've closed my eyes and said my prayers. I've gone through my mental to-do list, jotted everything down in my notebook.

Yet this bed has become a battering ocean. I flounder in it every night, struggling to stay afloat above the waves churning within me. That conversation. This email. What I didn't do, what I wanted to do but couldn't. How desperate I am for rest. If only I could get to shore, that elusive place where I am somehow carried to the refuge of sleep.

Instead, I'm tossed about far from comfort and release. The hours tick by, but I'm afraid to check the clock. I pull the covers up close to my chin, smooth my pillow, and press my cheek down into its soft billow.

I recite Scripture. Practice deep breathing. I try my best not to move. Even though it is quiet, my tears shake inside me because I know it's happening again.

Insomnia.

The Last Defense

Doesn't God give good sleep to those he loves? I ask myself.

And then it begins, the ways in which I accuse my heart. I sift through my world looking for a culprit, like a mad woman digging through the kitchen junk drawer to find a pen that works.

God, please. Let me sleep, I beg. Because if God is love and yet I'm not asleep, something must be wrong.

Sleeplessness feels shameful. It says I'm unlovable to God, guilty of not trusting him enough. I didn't understand that sleep doesn't always come easy—especially when God is carrying your heart on a journey to true spiritual rest.

One of the hardest whitespaces to fill with rest happens at night.

Sleep. It's the last defense our body has to let us know: something isn't right. Inside. We realize the storm isn't receding.

It dawns on us. Every plan we've held on to—along with the cargo we've been carrying—needs to be cut. All the provisions we purchased at great cost, packed and piled safely below, need to be let go.

We need to heave the cargo back up on deck. We must grab a friend next to us and shout against the gale of howling winds and scaling waves.

Help me. It's too heavy.

Help me. Throw this. Overboard.

It is time. We must shed everything for this life we steer to become lighter, to make it through the storm of stress.

Shedding

Just like the sailors caught in a violent storm with the apostle Paul had to do, we have to dump the cargo. They had to cut the ship's tackle by hand—flinging the very ropes and rigging *that once gave the sail speed and direction* into the violent waters of a storm.

The storm was so fierce they had to saw off the ropes that held the lifeboats and watch them plummet into the sea. We too must jettison the lifeboats we've constructed.

Luke, in his letter to Theopholis, says:

Since neither sun nor stars appeared for many days, and no small storm was assailing us, from then on all hope of our being saved was gradually abandoned. (Acts 27:20)

Luke and everyone else on that ship felt hopeless. Even though the captain and crew did what experience taught them, they still couldn't control the storm.

The storm of insomnia that renders us hopeless does *not* mean we have failed in our journey of faith. *It only means we are on a spiritual journey to create whitespace in our lives—to jettison the plans, people, and things we were never meant to carry.* We are in the process of shedding what makes our voyage too heavy.

God wants to hold us in the storm and whisper to us—

Nothing can stop my plans for you.
    Not bad luck. Bad health. Bad decisions.
    I will never leave you. I am faithful. I love you.

It's Jesus alive in you and me. The gospel. This is the story he's writing in us, right in the middle of the wreckage of life's storms.

What Really Matters

The chaos of sleep deprivation strips life down to the essentials. A life once focused on destination gets wiped out by what's elemental: eating, sleeping, drinking, making your bed, feeding the kids, and tucking them in at night with a story and a prayer. The simplest chores—laundry, grocery shopping, and cooking—are no longer incidental.

In the midst of the storm, Paul offers words of encouragement:

> Yet now I urge you to keep up your courage, for there will be *no loss of life* among you, but only of the ship. (v. 22)

Only the ship. I thought my relationship with God was what was wrong. I thought my faith was faulty. But God has been showing me insomnia isn't spiritual punishment.

Sleeplessness is a human experience where God meets with us. Shipwrecked by insomnia, I am still loved. I am still valued because God is still with me.

What must I shed to make it through? What is worth fighting to keep? Where is God and does he hear me? Uncovering these answers requires I take care of myself, because insomnia isn't an equation to be solved. Recovering sleep is a journey through the soul. It will take time.

This journey is also unpredictable because we have to do things we would rather avoid at all costs.

Self-Care: Whitespace on a Soul's Journey

Sleep isn't as simple as the articles on sleep hygiene make it out to be. Sometimes sleep goes beyond the discipline of getting to bed on time or avoiding workouts four hours before lights out. Left to my own devices, I definitely prefer *doing something* about my struggle to sleep—rather than *bringing my struggling self* to Jesus.

Self-care is a lot more intimate. It's more vulnerable to say

I need loving. I'm tired.
I can't do it all. I need others.
I'm not okay.

Sleeplessness is a soul's journey to find rest. Self-care is *one movement* in that journey to make room for whitespace and fill it with rest. Self-care is a step of faith to take care of our body and soul.

Nurturing my insomniac self has freed me to practice resting in God's love for me.

This is hard because I feel guilty focusing on me, but Hebrews 4:11 tells us to labor—*to exert all our energy*—to enter this rest.

It may feel selfish prioritizing our well-being because someone else's needs may not be met. It can involve major life changes. Dismantling our lifeboats and tossing our cargo overboard. It may be small, nuanced changes to take care of yourself. Every movement that gives your body a chance to heal gives your soul room to breathe.

Prioritizing self-care is an act of faith to tune your heart with God. In music, whitespace sits as a rest on a music sheet, marking an interval of silence. Breathing in a pause. It allows music to resonate in *beautiful harmony*. Your soul is an instrument of God's voice. Taking care of yourself nurtures the voice God placed in you.

Whitespace is also an act of faith to capture God's image in you. In photography, whitespace is used to create *movement*, evoking mood and emotion. Your soul is an artistic still. When we care for our well-being, our hearts become tender. We become *moveable*.

God can prompt us. Without whitespace, we become emotionally disconnected. We cannot be touched, nor can we touch anyone.

Because the focus of God's heart has always been your heart, self-care is really a soul's journey to fully receive his love.

A Promise: The Beloved

My journey to sleep signaled a new beginning: *becoming the beloved.*

Maybe Psalm 127:2, "For He gives to His beloved even in his sleep," isn't a true or false statement about God's love or an indictment on our faith. *Maybe this verse is a promise God makes to give us courage to investigate why we have insomnia, to surrender what we need to let go—because we are the beloved.*

As I realized finding sleep was going to be a long journey rather than a quick fix, insomnia prompted me to make movements of self-care in five ways.

Five Movements to Create Whitespaces of Self-Care

1. Signaling Rest to My Body

I had to learn to be kind to my body. This was a bizzarro world for me, because prior to PTSD I was in perfect health. I knew how to push my body to the max, but I didn't know how to care for it when it was weary.

I asked myself what I would do for a friend if she were feeling dizzy, nauseated, and sleep-deprived. I would buy her flowers. Give her bath gel with natural aromatherapy. Play soothing music in the evenings for her.

I'd take her on a walk outside to get some exercise. Encourage her to sit on a bench and feel the sun. I'd buy her a fuzzy bathrobe, even though it wasn't her birthday, because hers had been through two pregnancies and was way too old.

I took longer hot baths in the evening. I treated myself to the spa, even though it wasn't a special occasion. I turned off my computer after 5:00 p.m. to detox my mind from stress triggered by being online.

I did these things, knowing they wouldn't solve my insomnia, to signal rest to my body for the hard work of renovating my life.

2. Eating Healthy for Pleasure

I wanted to nourish my body, to relieve it from the stress of not eating well. Jesus cares about eating. When he raised the little girl who was dead, the first thing he said was, "Give the little girl something to eat."[1]

When I'm stressed, I skip meals or eat purely for functional reasons. I chew food without tasting it, gulp down water, or graze on carbs and junk food.

I'm reminded of the apostle Paul's words to the crew stranded in the storm:

> "You have been constantly watching and going without eating, having taken nothing. Therefore I encourage you to take some food." . . . Having said this, he took bread . . . and began to eat. (Acts 27:33–35)

I made myself sit when eating. Prepare a drink and eat fruit, veggies, and protein. Just like I do for my children. I played music if I was indoors to help set the mood.

Jesus took the time to stop and eat with Mary, Martha, and Lazarus. Somehow, eating with others was part of his journey. So I made a short list of friends to invite over for lunch or invite out for dinner.

3. Enjoying In-the-Skin Friends

When you're sick and dizzy, you need friends who can handle the weak you. The tired you. It's been surprising to find new friends I could simply hang out with, without having much to say. Without the pressure of conversation. These friendships have gone deep. These are friends I could invite over but cancel at the last minute if I didn't feel well. And they would understand.

I also reconnected with old friends, like Elaine, whom I hadn't seen in over a year. I told her I wanted to go out to dinner with her, but I might suddenly lose it and burst out crying. Would that scare her? She said no, so I started putting in my calendar: "Night out with Elaine."

I never did get through a meal without crying. But I'd go home thankful I was able to go out for Korean BBQ or sushi, even though

I must've looked like a wreck doing it. I was a lot happier having shared laughter too.

4. Extending Self-Compassion: Name Your Stress

When you make a mistake, when you don't feel like you're doing your best and you're failing—offer yourself the whitespace of self-compassion. To be human. To be loved.

Name your stress. I got this idea from Jesus's trip across a lake to the country of the Gerasenes just to free one man of his demons.[2] The man was so tortured he couldn't sleep at night either. He roamed the graveyards, cutting himself, in chains. There were so many demons this evil spirit even had a name. Legion.

A name? This bothered me. Why would the Bible legitimize something so terrible with a name?

I looked closer. *Jesus asked the evil spirit what his name was.* Jesus was the one who initiated this conversation. It is important to Jesus—naming what hurts us.

Jesus cares about the things that torture us. We can name our anxious thoughts with him. One by one. Over and again. He can handle it. He won't turn away.

Let's give ourselves compassion. Even if it causes swine to run themselves off the cliff and the village goes mad. We can trust that someone can be with us this way. As is.

5. Sharing My Story

Open up and investigate with others. Find others who recognize faith is organic, who are kind and gentle because they are in the process too. These are companions on the path of flesh and faith.

Be curious about other people's stories. Give others room to travel the whitespaces in their stories. Listen. Ask questions. You may find yourself in a conversation about their story that connects with yours.

Be curious about your own story. Find a therapist to help you ask the right questions, to navigate the mysteries of your wounding and your healing. Finding the right therapist is a lot like dating. Expect "bad dates." Keep looking until you find someone with the gift of counsel, experienced in the unique story you're piecing together.

Beautiful Seed

Sleeplessness is one of the most treacherous terrains we may be called to navigate. Everything we've worked hard to plant and till in the soil of our lives by faith may look barren. But even in the storm of troubled sleep, God is alive and faithful to make something beautiful out of us.

He's done it from the beginning of time and his fingers continue to gently trace his image in us. We may lie awake in the dark, with tears shed so many times we can no longer cry. We don't need to understand how it will happen, how he can carry us through this nightmare of anguished wakefulness.

It doesn't matter. Because whether waking or sleeping, God won't abandon us.

And the last of the grain that took a whole season of harvesting, the one we lost in the storm?

He's going to replenish it all.[3]

He's carrying us in his arms, no matter how bruised or broken we feel. He's planting beautiful seed for our journey—seed that's thriving even among the barren months of sleep that alludes us. That seed is Jesus. Alive in us. As is.

Let's make room for this seed of rest to grow. To create whitespace for people, places, and pastimes that are healing, nurturing, and caring for our hearts and bodies. So we can testify we are women who are daughters of a loving Father. So we can rest in this journey of faith when sleep doesn't come easy.

Space for self-care. To investigate. To be the beloved. Today.

One of the first places I started shedding cargo was clutter. It was growing in my heart and spilling out into my home.

The Kingdom of God is like a farmer who scatters seed on the ground. Night and day, while he's asleep or awake, the seed sprouts and grows, but he does not understand how it happens. All by itself the soil produces grain. (Mark 4:26–27 NLT; v. 28 NIV)

Pull Up a Chair—Share

What keeps you up at night?

How is God guiding you on the journey to find rest through sleep?

A Whitespace Prompt—Try This

Rank your list. Which whitespaces of self-care are you craving most? Rank them 1 to 5.

Signaling rest to my body
Eating healthy for pleasure
Enjoying in-the-skin friends
Extending self-compassion
Sharing my story

Small movements. What small movements can you make this week for your top pick? Resist the urge to check them off. Just make a movement in that direction. Remember rest is a journey, not a checkbox.

Soul Conversation—Confide in Him

Where have the waves in life led you? Is there cargo to shed or lifeboats to release? What is worth fighting to keep?

9

clutter

Letting Go

There are far, far better things ahead than any
we leave behind.

C. S. Lewis

It started off as a project to help de-stress my hubby.

I wanted to do something loving, to show my gratitude for all
he's done for me. After all, helping someone recover from post-
traumatic stress disorder can be . . . well . . . *stressful.*

Can you imagine seeing the one you love struggle through physical and emotional hardship day in and day out?

It would tear at your heart, breaking it a little more every time
you relived a painful memory through her eyes, as she recounted
each story to you unguarded. What would it be like working a full
day's job at the office only to return home to help with the kids,

getting sleep sliced up by tending to wake-ups, then rising early to ready the kids for school to ease your wife's burdens?

The journey to love someone as she heals calls a husband to give everything in his power to take care of his wife. He will keep going, even when his heart and body tell him he should rest too, even as love takes a toll on him as well.

Out the Window

I searched my mind for something I could offer my husband—as a token of my appreciation for the journey he's been on to walk with me through healing.

One idea immediately jumped into my mind. *Clutter.*

I wanted to get rid of clutter because trying to recover from PTSD basically throws housework out the window. Housecleaning is not one of my love languages. I am clean, but I organize my life in neat piles. *I know where everything is. Just don't touch my piles.*

My husband, on the other hand, is the super neat, no-stacking-allowed type. He views the words *piles* and *organized* as an oxymoron, while they co-exist in a symbiotic relationship in my world.

I decided one Saturday morning to do something about the growing clutter. It had gotten to a level where it stressed out even me. I wanted to speak his love language. I needed to get rid of stuff.

Should Save and Might Need

The hallway between the kids' bedroom and ours had become lined with overflowing laundry baskets. Downstairs in the dining room, more stacks waited to be "processed." The same thing started happening in my living room. The family room. Then the garage.

There was no more space to stuff things to put away "later." I could hardly open the drawers of my desk. Cleaning up became a major chore. After a Herculean effort of Tetris-like maneuvers, I'd make a clearing. But it'd only last a few days. Clutter explosion. Again.

Laundry reached an out-of-control status. The kids started pulling clothes out of the dryer in the morning to get dressed. Every day started with a crisis, combing through laundry to find matching socks.

I tried to de-clutter many times. I'd drag stuff out of my closets to make a Goodwill pile. But every time I took something out, I'd find a reason to keep it. Pieces of red rock to remind me of the year I hiked Sedona in the moonlight. Seashells I've culled along beaches over the years.

Things I bought because I planned to do something with them later. Jell-O molds I thought were so cute, sitting in my pantry with tags still on. The big black scrapbook I imagined creating with the boys, untouched.

Maybe so-and-so would like this.

I should save it.

I might need it later.

I'd move it back to the "keep" pile. Two hours later, I'm left with a mountain of stuff to keep and an anthill's worth for Goodwill. Then I'd blow another couple hours getting everything squeezed back into the closet.

I was frantic with stress. I wasn't making any room for whitespace or movements of rest.

Something Drastic

Eric calls my clean-up efforts archeological digs, with various items recovered from different epochs of my life. Pre-mom. Pre-married. Boys'-baby-years. Newlywed. Work-years.

I wasted so many weekends failing to de-clutter. I had to do something drastic. I called my high school best friend, Annette.

Annette's the only person I know now who's been in the house I grew up in. She's seen the greasy kitchen walls, the mildewed bathroom tiles, and my locker-sized closet. She's seen the mess and she still stayed my friend.

Annette was always neat and organized. Her bedroom was bigger than our living room. She had beautiful bedroom furniture that matched and a huge closet filled with peach, pink, and pastels, squarely folded.

She has three kids now. She lives a few cities away, so we don't get to see each other often. But every time I've stopped by, she always has everything beautifully and simply arranged.

I called her. "Annette. You have to help me."

"What is it?" She sounded concerned.

"I need to get rid of stuff. I can't stand the clutter anymore. It's out of control. Stressing me out. I'm sure it's killing Eric."

"Yeah . . ." Annette agrees.

"I've had this stuff for decades. You've got to be brutal with me, Annette." I gave her a mission. "Come look at my stuff. Tell me what needs to go."

It was time to purge.

Never could I have guessed an innocent project would unfurl painful flashes of what it means to let go in order to be loved. To live as the beloved daughter of God.

Memories

I walked Annette through my house, top to bottom. I opened every closet to show her the horror of mishmashed objects, so she could survey the damage. I opened kitchen cabinets, bedroom dresser, and desk drawers.

For the first time in my life, I allowed someone to look at all the spaces I tucked stuff away. I was holding my breath, waiting

106

for her to shrink back in horror. Instead, my friend looked at me with calm confidence.

"This is good, Bonnie. You have a lot of space," Annette commented. "Let's tackle the kids' stuff first."

Annette started culling the children's books I stored in every room. "Why don't we gather all the kids' books and put them in their bookcase?"

I began to feel anxious. Dizzy. Nauseated even. My breath started quickening. I told her there wasn't enough room in the bookcase for all the kids' books. Annette flipped through some baby books and asked why I still kept them. Caleb was already four and Josh was seven.

I told her it's sentimental, recounting a memory for each book.

"Bonnie. You don't need a book to remind you." Annette looked straight at me. "The memories are in your heart."

Room for Now

Annette suggested I save a few things that were special in a memory box for each child. "We're only going to keep enough books that fit on these bookshelves."

Then she found books from my childhood. "Do you ever read these?" I didn't. I kept quiet about the other boxes of books I've lugged around for years.

"Let's go through them. You're gonna make room for your life *now*. Okay?" She spoke ever so gently, but I began to cry.

"What's wrong?" Annette started organizing piles of *Keep* versus *Get Rid Of*.

"I want to keep these," I took the books from her. I suddenly didn't want any more de-cluttering.

Annette's eyes turned to meet mine. "What's happening, Bonnie? What memories are you attaching to these books?"

I didn't know what to say. I couldn't describe the weight of anxiety tearing at my heart. I remembered how these books felt in my hands as a little girl. My treasured collection. The few things that were mine.

I used to read them under the blanket with a dimming flashlight, while my mom yelled at me from outside the bedroom door. How I'd come up for air the minute she flew into the room. I'd hide my books under my pillow or drop them to the side of the bed if she came near. How cut-up I felt whenever she'd assault me with words like ammo.

I'd listen for the click of her bedroom door to close. Then I'd flip to the page where I left off. I'd read and it would push out all the ugly words that lashed into my heart. The words on those pages wrapped around my soul like papier-mâché.

Annette put her hand on mine as my tears dropped. "Your boys are going to enjoy new books with you. You don't need these anymore." She placed her other hand firmly on the "Goodbye" books pile.

What Was Missing

"What's under here?" Annette asked, poking in the space under my dresser that was crammed with thin metal and wooden things.

"Picture frames," I answered, pulling out silver, antique white, three-photo, collage, and single photo frames. In different shapes and sizes. Some were empty, ones I'd bought but never used. Some were old, still holding photos I'd never changed.

"Why do you have so many?" Annette couldn't understand. We counted more than twenty.

I hardly ever had my school pictures taken. The teacher would pass them out, calling out names. I'd see my friends get excited, huddling around each other's desks, pulling out those glossy sheets. I'd go home and cry.

Most of my treasured childhood moments never made it to celluloid. It cost money to have a camera, money to develop the film. And photos weren't a priority.

It seems so trivial, I hesitate to even write about it. But a picture tells me a moment existed, that something was worth remembering. That someone was cherished.

Not the Stuff

"I'm seeing a pattern," Annette sighed. "Memories. You don't need frames to hold on to them. Make new ones."

Four hours later, I helped Annette load bags of stuff into the back of her SUV. "Just put them in my car. I'll take them to Goodwill," I offered.

"I'm leaving with all this stuff today, Bonnie." She hugged me and told me how proud she was of me. As I watched Annette's car leave, a lump of panic dropped into my stomach. I called her an hour later. I wanted the white picture frame with the dotted ribbing. Could she save it for me?

She texted back. She had already stopped by Goodwill on the way home. Everything was gone.

That night, and for the next few days thereafter, panic attacks fired up my body, disrupting my sleep. Dr. P says I would've probably developed OCD over the years. I'd eventually hoard, if I hadn't gone through the pain and panic of letting clutter go.

"It's not the stuff you're attached to," he explains. "It's the *avoidance of pain*. The fear of saying goodbye. Of facing what comes after."

The Stress of Avoidance

Jesus wants us to make room for our lives today.

Jesus wants us to have whitespace. In the closet. On the shelves. In our hearts and in our homes.

In order to find freedom in *who we are now*, we must undergo the anxiety of letting go of *who we've been*. It's the fear of being in need, the empty spaces we want to avoid. We tell ourselves we need to save. We might need it later.

But the stress of avoidance causes anxiety.

I think about the widow making Elijah a meal with the last of her flour.[1] She didn't save it. She poured it away. Would God provide again?

Whitespace: a Soulful Home

Rest is a journey of your soul *now*. Not yesterday. With the new space opening up in my house, I'm taking a new journey: *to a soulful home.*

What colors feel restful and happy?

How can my home reflect beauty?

What are a few simple things that reflect God's story in me?

How can I create an inviting space for family and friends?

I still miss my old things, but they are gone. So I look to the whitespace around me.

I'm learning to give myself permission to explore who I am as the beloved. A rest is used in music to give resonance to beautiful harmony, and I am learning to make my home a restful sanctuary for the soul. Whitespace in the home allows for movement and relaxation, creating a peaceful space for life today. Where I can breathe. Physically. Emotionally. Spiritually. With God. And others.

Let's create whitespace in our homes. Let's say goodbye in order to say hello to *the journey of becoming the beloved.* Making room for a soulful home.

More Than an Organizational Project

De-cluttering became more than an organizational project. De-cluttering freed up space in my soul to awaken rest.

Getting rid of clutter is not easy. Letting go involves looking at what you're holding on to and why. Sometimes, it's time to say goodbye to what once gave you comfort, so you can face the place of empty and surrender yourself to what your heart truly longs for.

It's what Jesus is whispering to me—

Yes. I know.
 I have more than this.
 For you.

More than this? So I asked Annette to come back to de-clutter my bedroom. I didn't think any more pain was left until we moved a bookcase.

> So do not fear, for I am with you;
>> do not be dismayed, for I am your God.
> I will strengthen you and help you;
>> I will uphold you with my righteous right hand.
> (Isa. 41:10 NIV)

Pull Up a Chair—Share

How is God prompting you to create a more restful space at home for your soul?

A Whitespace Prompt—Try This

Volunteer your friend. Know someone who is kind, with a natural affinity for organizing a simple, restful home environment?

111

Take a risk and enlist her help to be brutally honest and gently de-clutter.

Bite-size de-cluttering. Break up the de-cluttering project into bite-size pieces. My effort ended up taking six weekends: family room/dining room/the kids' bedrooms, master bedroom, garage, laundry area, living room, and kitchen.

Follow Annette's Three Rules to De-clutter (approved by Dr. P):
1. Only keep what I use/need now (or the foreseeable near future).
2. Only keep/store what I have shelf/floor space for. One type of item per storage space.
3. Let go of anything you haven't used in a year.

Take pictures of what is harder to let go. Capture memories in a journal.

Keep a list of soulful home ideas you've always wanted to try.

Saving things to pass on to others, but never do so? Load them up and drop them off today. Otherwise, cut your losses. Donate to Goodwill. That's what I had to do.

Donate the items you've been putting aside to sell on eBay or Craigslist. Keeping stuff in a holding area costs more than money: your rest.

A Soul Conversation—Confide in Him

What are you afraid to say goodbye to?

Are you facing what comes after?

Share the memories or thoughts that won't let go of your heart and allow God to hold you.

10

the bookcase

Moving Things

We can never give up longing and wishing while
we are still alive. There are certain things we feel
to be beautiful and good, and we must hunger
for them.

T. S. Eliot

Annette asked me why I had my bookcase in my bedroom. I tell
her that's just the way it's always been. I like my books near me.

Annette looked at the corner of the room, where my six-shelf
bookcase covered the wall.

"You'd open up a lot of space if you moved your bookcase somewhere else. How about the living room? It would look great there."

"No." It was not up for discussion.

I've always had my books near me. They were my safety. No
matter where I was—growing up as a little girl, pressed into my

college dorm room, or sharing an apartment with my mother and sister as a young adult—my bookcase, desk, and bed composed the one space that belonged to me.

"Let's just see what it looks like," Annette prods. "Your bedroom should be a sanctuary. Restful. You can still have the books you're reading next to you." She pointed to the stack on my nightstand. "I'll move things back if you don't like it. Okay?"

With that, Annette started relocating the books. I had to pick up the boys from school, so I couldn't stop her. When I returned, I was surprised. I actually liked how my books looked in the living room, next to the window overlooking the sun and trees in the backyard.

This isn't just a living room anymore. It struck me. *This is now my living room.*

On my way upstairs, Annette walks down with the last of my books in her arms. "Check it out. Your room."

My room did look bigger. There was more whitespace. I liked it. A lot.

Little did I know later that night, and every night for the next few days, my body would be terrorized by flashbacks and panic attacks. It was the same scene that kept firing up.

I was trapped. Pinned down. In a bed.

A Fish Flapping

It wasn't my bed. My mother opened a fast-food Chinese to-go restaurant when I was ten years old. *Combination #1 Beef or Chicken Chow Mein with Egg Roll. Combination #2 BBQ Pork or Chicken Fried Rice. . . .*

My mother threw a wok over flames to fill the orders, handled the cash register, and worked the sink and dishes. She worked really late into the night. She arranged for us to stay at another family's house until she closed up shop and picked us up past midnight.

We'd eat dinner with them but I felt awkward there. The mom would tell me not to eat too much. *Save some for others.* They were an older couple with five children. One was a teenage boy.

There was a bunk bed in his room. I would sleep on the top bunk before my mother came. One night, as I was lying there, I felt someone near me. His hand slipped under the covers. He was touching me. In places he shouldn't. I didn't know about the birds and the bees.

He stood there, over me, his face inches from mine. He was soothing my hair with his hand. He whispered firmly, "Shh . . . everything's okay. It's just me."

I said, "Stop it." I tried to push his hand away, twist my body to get up. But he wouldn't let me. His fingers pressed down on me. Hard. Digging into my bone. He was hurting me.

I started to cry. He cupped my mouth and said, "No, no. Shh . . . you'll wake everyone up. Quiet."

My neck, body, arms tightened, wild with fear. I tried to break out of his grip by pushing my heels against the mattress, to get up on my legs. But I felt like a fish flapping its fins in vain on butcher paper against the force of his strength.

"Relax." I'd forgotten how evil and creepy his voice sounded.

Unable to escape, I just laid there, waiting for it to be over. It happened a few more times. Then I refused to go to bed.

You're Fine

I told his two older sisters what happened, but they didn't believe me. They told me I was imagining it. A dream.

I was afraid to tell his mom, so I told my mother. On the car ride there, I told her he touched me. More than once. At night when I went to bed.

"Are you sure? Did he do anything else?" she asked.

115

"No, he didn't do anything else." I was confused. I thought what he did was bad.

I'll never forget what my mother said next. "He's a teenager. He's curious. That's all. Just stay away from him."

I did. I watched my back. Whenever I knew he was coming into the room, I'd go to another.

Nothing really happened. You're fine, I've always told myself.

It hadn't bothered me since I was ten years old. Every now and then, it crossed my mind if I heard something in the news or saw a scene in a movie. But I never dwelt on it. Jesus already brought me through it. I'm already a victor in Christ, right?

Then why was this memory popping up *now*—now that I'm walking into the restful whitespace of my bedroom, smiling as sunlight reflects on the wall where my bookcase once stood?

It is because whitespace frees us to face the truth about ourselves and this truth sets us free. When we make room for whitespace, we have to move things. We are changing how we've always done things. We uncover layers of ourselves we had to put to the side in order to deal with the stress at hand.

The part of us who wants to have a choice becomes free. To have a voice and a say in the matter.

Who are the people in your life who encourage your voice to surface? How often do we find ourselves minimizing our choices?

We don't have to be trapped in how things ought to be, because Jesus frees us to take shelter in him.

> Christ has set us free to live a free life. So take your stand! Never again let anyone put a harness of slavery on you. (Gal. 5:1 Message)

Whitespace: Making Choices

Experiencing rest is freedom. But freedom isn't a spiritual light switch. We have to make choices and exercise that freedom. We need to value our hearts as much as Jesus does. God gave us free will to make choices and grace when we make mistakes. To learn what we like. And what we don't.

The act of making our own decisions is an act of faith, because we are choosing to voice what God puts on our souls.

> Do not work for food that spoils; instead, work for the food that lasts for eternal life . . . food the Son of Man will give you. (John 6:27 GNT)

The crowds didn't feel comfortable with choice. They responded to Jesus by asking, "Just tell us. What exactly does God want us to do?"

Instead of spelling out what to do, Jesus invited them to choose. Jesus answered, "What God wants you to do is to believe in the one he sent. . . . I am the living bread. Eat this bread." People were appalled. "This teaching is too hard. Who can listen to it?" So many disciples following Jesus left him that day.[1]

The journey of spiritual whitespace isn't static. *Whitespace is movement.* To make the radical choice to leave the louder clamoring voices, in order to follow the one, quiet Voice inside. To follow Jesus further, we need to move things. We need to make changes to mark God's love for us.

One Phrase

"I just won't write." That's what I told Dr. P when we processed this terrible memory. If writing is what triggered this Pandora's Box of memories, then the most logical thing to do was to stop writing. *Perfect. It's decided. I'll quit. It's not worth it.*

What difference would it make if I shut down the blog and said goodbye? In the big picture, it won't really matter whether I ever write a single word again. I'm not published. I had just one radio interview for an article I wrote once. I think I blabbed on too long. It never aired. Writing was good when it brought me joy. Now it's too hard. Too painful.

But the truth of the matter is this: I don't want to be the PTSD girl. "Ask Jesus," Dr. P replies. "What does he think?"

You are my beloved. I shake my head because it doesn't make sense. Every time I woke up reliving this disgusting memory of being trapped on that terrible bed with that terrible person, I heard this one phrase.

My beloved.

It's disorienting. The only two times the heavenly Father spoke to Jesus in the Gospels, he said, "You are my beloved, in whom I am well-pleased" (Matt. 3:17; 17:5). Why in the world would God say this to me now—messed up like this?

Beloved

Is God calling you to something that feels too hard? Are you struggling to understand how to walk the everyday while holding your dreams in one hand and the reality of your circumstances in the other?

Is there something you desire or fear that is so painful you don't know if you should hold on tighter or let it go entirely?

To avoid the hardness of the journey, you may be tempted, as I have been, to deny yourself the permission

to feel,

to dream, or

to grieve.

Jesus turns to us and tenderly whispers—

Live as my beloved. Lay your heart bare with me.

When you hear these words, take a step closer—even if it takes you beyond your place of control, into a place of faith—where

118

you are under the control of God's love and timetable, purposed for you.

This is what I am choosing, as I write to you in the dark with Jesus holding my hand. I am asking for *the courage to trust there are no mistakes in his timing. I am choosing to embrace this chapter he has allowed to take shape in my story today.*

I will not turn away. Don't turn away.

Who I Really Am

"You can try to stop writing," Dr. P offers. "But I don't think you can. When you write, you are at home with Jesus. You in Jesus. Jesus in you."

It got me thinking. *Maybe PTSD isn't who I really am. Maybe it's just what I'm walking through. Maybe "beloved" is who I am.*

I began wondering. How would life look as the beloved? What are the small, imperfect movements I can take to be free, as the beloved?

This is why I choose to write, even if it means I'll feel broken for a season. Because the other side of brokenness is restoration; the hope—the journey—is wholeness.

Let's choose freedom. Let's move things and make room for whitespace. Let's grow as the beloved. Just as we are.

The choices I started making were small. One in particular came in the size of a pastry glazed in old Chinatown.

Pull Up a Chair—Share

What new choices can you make to reclaim life the way God intended for you?

A Whitespace Prompt—Try This

Get "beloved" ideas. What are some projects or interests you want to look into, no matter how small or how "not you" they seem? God uses even the smallest movement. Like moving a bookcase from one place to another.

Ask yourself. What parts of you have you minimized that need attention, interest, and time to nurture?

A Soul Conversation—Confide in Him

Is there a painful scene in your life you've never let out into the light? It isn't who you are now, but you've had to survive it. Invite Jesus into that scene now. Write what happens there.

If you think of someone to share that scene with, write her name down. Ask God if he wants you to share it, and at some point to prompt you. Then leave it in his hands. In his time, he will.

11

pastry
Slow Eating

All you need is love. But a little chocolate now
and then doesn't hurt.

Charles Schultz

Buttery. Flaky. Sweet.

My mother would take my hand and we would wind our way
down the streets of Chinatown. San Francisco sits on ascending
shelves of weathered Victorian flats, lined with sheets of canopied
storefronts. The awnings jutting over wooden crates of dimpled
papaya next to mounds of googly-eyed flat fish stood like shade
trees in my concrete world.

I hated having to thread through the smelly open-air market
street they call Stockton. But if we wanted to get to *Ping Yuen* down
on Grant below us—if we wanted to get to the bakery—that's the
way we had to go.

That's how I first learned Chinese. I heard it spoken by Momma.

I'd look up at the signs perched vertically on storefronts. I'd see fiery Chinese characters, written in calligraphy brushstrokes.

I'd recognize one that looked like a sword pointing downward, flanked by two staccato marks, like wayward pearls of rice stuck on the rim of my bowl. *Ping.* It means "quiet, safety." The second character, *yuen*, is a box drawn like a picture frame, with bamboo shoot strokes arranged within. *Yuen* means "garden."

Ping Yuen. Quiet Safe Garden. We had arrived. Momma would open the door and I'd step into the warmth of the bakery, swathed in the scents of steaming egg custards still hot to the touch and dough rising in the oven on slats of baking sheets. I'd get right up close to the glass countertop display and stare into caramelized macaroon puffs, vanilla crème-swirled cakes, and coconut toasted breads. A parade of baked heaven.

It's a Chinese bakery, so there are yelps into the kitchen for more "*don tat!*" (egg tarts). Old men hard of hearing holler for "*gai mae bao!*" (rooster-tail buns, which the English call hot cross buns).

I always chose the same thing. Nestled in its own little aluminum foil pan was a perfect round half of a peach. It shimmered in a sweet glaze, sitting on a bed of light puff pastry.

A peach tart. It's my favorite thing in the whole wide world. Because for an unexplained space in time, my momma and I would sit at the café. She would buy one just for me.

My momma would smile. She would be happy. The world was all at once sweet and safe.

A Moment in Eternity

It always felt like an eternity, sitting there. Each bite was crispy. Pastry flakes would stick on my fingers and the peach never slid off, even though it felt smooth between my teeth as I bit into it. It would always last. It was good to me. It's no surprise decades later I would fall in love sitting across from Eric at a café on our first date.

No matter what stage of life I found myself in—cramming for mid-terms as a college student or enjoying a cappuccino with a book as a thirty-something single—enjoying something sweet at a café was my refuge. There's something about a pastry that is oh-so-comforting. You sit. You breathe.

I wonder if that's how Jesus felt about bread.

As a child, when he saw his mother knead and bake, did he feel the comfort of home? As the family gathered to pray and to dip bread in olive oil, did he feel safety, the peace of resting?

I think he did.

As Jesus looked into the faces of a crowd following him for days, the Scriptures tell us Jesus was moved with compassion. He felt their hunger. He did not want them to travel hurried and empty. He was afraid they would faint from the journey. He asked everyone to sit down.

This is what I imagine Jesus saying to the crowd near twilight, when everyone must have been confused about whether they should stay or go, whether there would be food or not—

There is a long journey ahead of you. Many days' worth.
Put down your things and watch the sun set with me.

And for a moment, everyone stopped. Jesus took some bread and broke it. Slowly, it made its way around.

Jesus must have sat there out in the open air, heart happy. Because for one meal, an eternity of happiness must have touched his soul, watching people taking time to sit together, relax, and eat. The compassion Jesus felt in the pit of his stomach wasn't just for their hunger, but for their journey.

Something Warm

Following Jesus through the land of anxiety and stress has been wearying. I don't have much of an appetite. Nothing looks all that appealing. But there is one scene from a story that keeps me company as I lie on my bed, struggling to gather my heart, get up, and prepare a meal for my family.

It's Jesus, up in the quiet, early morning.

He's been resurrected. He endured the most brutal form of execution, and he's got the scars and wounds to show for it. He must have had so much to tell his friends because they had given up hope.

The disciples had gone back to their old life of fishing: routine and monotony. Chores and repetition. Except no matter how hard they worked or how late they stayed, there was no fish.

Until Jesus arrived. Then their nets were full to overflowing.

Jesus gathered some stones. He made a fire.

Jesus knew what they liked best. He knew how they liked their fish cooked. How to best wash it, salt it. How to gently wait and watch it cook, until the skin tightened and crisped ever so slightly, because it meant the flesh was growing tender and sweet underneath.

He could have turned stones to bread. Fast. Easy. Instead Jesus placed the bread next to the fish, so it would soften and warm to their fingertips.

When they landed, [the disciples] saw a fire of burning coals there with fish on it, and some bread. (John 21:9 NIV)

Jesus looked into their eyes. He understood the devastation and helplessness they held in the pit of their stomachs.

Jesus says to you and me now—as he said to the disciples that quiet morning—

Come.
  Have breakfast.
Come.
  And eat. As is.
  Something warm. Slow. Something you like.

Slow Whitespace

Take the time to remember what you like.

Take the time to bake it. Prepare it. Cook it.

Enjoy and savor it. Slowly.

Drive out farther than usual. Go to that fruit stand where the cherries are darkest and sweetest. Take that trip across town and slip into that café with the perfect apple strudel, folded just the way you like.

Spend the extra time to chop fresh basil into that weekly pasta. Buy a block of cheese. Just this once. So you can grate it fresh on top. It will look pretty. Just because.

It is in that slow whitespace you'll be extending yourself the compassion Jesus would. If he could be there in person, he'd be there cooking for you. In your kitchen.

At the deli, there is slow whitespace there too, where the minestrone tastes especially good. Don't forget that special artichoke pasta salad, tossed with diced red peppers and a sweet vinaigrette.

Jesus knows.

Jesus cares.

Taking the extra time to care for our palates. Stopping to eat and nourish our bodies.

With good food. With space to pick up a fork and eat slowly. To give ourselves enough time to sip instead of gulp.

Slow Eating

It's a new kind of whitespace Jesus is showing me through my post-traumatic stress disorder.

Slow.

I wish I could tell you I discovered slow eating, slow cooking, and slow drinking out of a commitment to do life slower. That wouldn't be honest. I cannot move through my day as I used to. My desire for slow emerged out of desperation. To show myself the compassion Jesus longs for me to experience.

Make time to be with me this way, Jesus softly prompts. *Be kind. And compassionate. With yourself.*

What do you want to eat? What do you crave?

Make the room fragrant with food as it cooks. Look at how the colors change and how the juices bubble.

Make that pot of tea. Let it steep. Then pour it slowly.

We can rest with Jesus in slow whitespace—caring for our spirit by nourishing our bodies.

Slow. Quiet safety. *Ping yuen.*

Whitespace at the Table

I'm taking the time to set the table. To enjoy the pretty water goblets I used to save for guests. I use them for my family, for me. No special occasion.

I buy flowers. Not every week, but every couple weeks or so. I used to buy them only when friends came over.

But now I'm thinking differently. I see whitespace at the table.

Candles. Just because they're pretty. They remind me of what it might have been like. To eat with Jesus. To see him across the glow of a table and hear him say a prayer. I want to create these memories at the table with my children.

The food can be simple. It's the dinner conversation that sets the pace for whitespace at the table as a family. Sometimes, Hubby and I want some extra whitespace as a couple midweek. So we eat after we tuck the kids into bed and enjoy an in-house dinner date night.

I want that spiritual whitespace. Found between bread and wine, the presence of Jesus.

Time Well Spent

On days my anxiety is especially bad, the only whitespace I experience might be driving my kids to a park, unpacking turkey and cheese sandwiches and Goldfish. Basking in sunshine or bundled warm in the cold, my boys see their mommy smile.

Sometimes the biggest things I've done in one day is eating, breathing, and drinking enough water. *Is this what my life has come down to?* I sigh.

Then I think of Jesus. He could have done so much more that early morning years ago. He could have accomplished a lot of big things, having come back from the dead—places to go and people to see.

Instead Jesus took time to be with his friends. Sit at the water's edge. Cook. And simply eat. Taking time to nourish their bodies.

It's time well spent together, Jesus gently assures me.

On difficult days, remember the whitespace of *ping yuen*, quiet safety nestled in the garden of your heart.

Sip. Taste. Smell. Savor. In between bites, Jesus meets with us.

Because the journey ahead is long, stop. Offer yourself the space to pause. Invite another into that space. Even for a bite of pastry. The moment is worth it.

Because sometimes the one thing that strengthens our hearts when we're stressed is the company of a trusted friend. That's why I was so desperate when I made a phone call early one morning.

Pull Up a Chair—Share

How can you rest with Jesus through slow whitespace at your table, cooking or eating?

A Whitespace Prompt—Try This

Al fresco whitespace. Do as Jesus did. How can you enjoy food or a cup of coffee with a view outside? Drive to a nearby park or a favorite café, or snuggle up outside on your porch.

Slow eating. Enjoy food sitting down. Choose to eat something that is warm, that takes longer to eat.

Slow cooking. What is a yummy recipe you haven't made in a million years—or a new one to try?

Slow friendship. Go out to eat with an old friend. Have coffee with a new friend.

Don't skip. Don't skip lunch. Or breakfast. Enjoy sipping something warm. Hot.

Slow fruit. Make yourself a fruit salad. Go to the farmers' market. Take the time to pick the darker cherries out of the red.

Slow ambience. Dust off those candles. Buy those flowers. Just this once. Set them at your table. Enjoy.

A Soul Conversation—Confide in Him

Think back. What are your earliest memories of food and the warmth it offered you?

Where were you and how did it feel?

12

the phone call

Friendship

A friend is that other person with whom we can
share our solitude. We don't have to say or do
something special.

Henri Nouwen

I was feeling desperate.

So I called her. I didn't know why it was happening. Only that
it was.

A panic attack. It hit me, like a tsunami punching through whatever inside me held me together. Choking tears erupted so deeply I
couldn't inhale. Stabbing fear poured through. Whatever captured
me before was here to carry me away in its clutches again.

This was before I found Dr. P, so I didn't know I was experiencing PTSD. I felt like a passenger on the *Titanic*. The stern of my
soul started to tip and I was sliding. I felt an unexplainable need

to hold on to someone in the skin who could hear my voice and I could hear hers.

I didn't want to call my husband. He was at work. A heavy day of meetings. I knew I'd scare him into coming home. So I called the first person I thought of, another stay-at-home mom, a friend who had known me since I was single.

I dialed her number, praying she'd pick up.

"Hello?" *Oh good. She's there.* I broke down bawling at the sound of her voice.

I sputter, struggling to get the words out. "I'm not doing good. At all . . ." I didn't have words yet to describe what was happening. "I don't want to be alone right now. Can I come over?"

"What's wrong?" she asked.

"I don't know why . . ." I was afraid to say, "I'm having panic attacks."

"I'm actually out taking a walk right now." Her voice trails.

I felt awkward. "That's okay." I sniffled. "Can I come over later— in the afternoon?" I didn't want to be at home alone with the boys. If I could find somewhere to go for a few hours, Eric would be home and I'd be okay.

"I'm so sorry, Bonnie. This afternoon isn't going to work." She encouraged me to take care of myself. But she was sorry. She had to go.

That's how we ended the phone call. She never called back to check on me. Never invited me to come over later. She hasn't called me since.

Sometimes, when we feel most overwhelmed, we can find ourselves alone, with no one to turn to.

Have you ever felt lost, unable to find someone to keep company with you in your time of need? Have you felt the awkward silence filling the space as you struggle to give voice to your need?

I'm learning not everyone can touch that place of empty. *Not everyone knows how to stay.* Not everyone can travel alongside you when the journey of rest takes you down dark and deep valleys.

But it doesn't mean our search for friendship needs to end fruitless.

Whitespace of Friendship

Open-heart vulnerability. We seek a deeper level of friendship when stress and anxiety hit us. We seek friends who are not afraid of vulnerability, friends who meet us heart to heart.

Being known. This is what we find in the whitespace of friendship. Vulnerability is what our souls need to rest.

This journey to discover friendship begins the way a white dandelion puff sheds its seeds into the wind. By gently letting go. It takes courage to step out into the *whitespace of friendship*, not knowing whether someone's heart will open and give us a place to rest.

To find that open-heart vulnerability, we take the first step. To share our story. To risk rejection and see if another will hear and echo their stories in return.

The whitespace of friendship—*of open-heart vulnerability*—is where my story took a turn.

Challenge to Stay

You see, when I was a twentysomething with dreams in her eyes, I left my Silicon Valley career and ventured into the mission field. But when I returned unexpectedly, my bags were packed with hurt and betrayal.

I tried to open them up to friends back home but I was met with silence and disappointment. I was no longer the happy Bonnie everyone had known. They didn't know what to say. I had hard questions, but they were only comfortable with simple answers.

Their rejection launched me into a season of hiding for many years.

That experience taught me not to trust myself—or others—with the parts of me that were unfinished. I hid my brokenness for years. But when I started struggling with panic attacks, I wanted to go a different route.

I longed to open up and find real friendship. Was I really destined to journey alone, or can what I've taught others come true for me? Can Jesus love me through others, broken?

To find out, I had to risk and be vulnerable. My challenge in community was to stay present in my story, no matter where my search led.

The Broken Message of Family

I made a list of people to confide in. I told myself I would keep going down this list until I found someone. I braced myself and started dialing.

I called Merrianne. I hadn't seen her in years. She was my junior high Sunday school teacher, the first person to disciple me. She'd sat across from me in our grimy, dimpled-floor kitchen. It was a two-person book club, really. We'd talk through book topics and pray.

Even though I trusted her with a lot of my secrets, I never told Merrianne how dysfunctional my family life was growing up, how truly lonely and sad I was.

It was a family code I never wanted to break.

Never talk bad about your family. Ever.

The shame of coming from a broken family seeped into my faith. I never wanted to be seen as ungrateful to God. I kept quiet. *But what I was really doing was ignoring my heart, rather than facing the truth.*

I couldn't cover up the cracks anymore. There comes a point in our stories when we can't see the beautiful side of renovation. We only see the tearing down. This is the time we truly walk by faith, by confessing what we fear most: we do not have the emotional resources. *We can't go it alone.* We need others to be God's voice and heart to us.

The old messages from our broken families of origin teach us the safest place is to suffer alone. To keep silent and never rock the boat. To never need—to keep doing the same thing and hope that it gets better.

That's why I called Merrianne. I surrendered to my need. I cried into the phone. *I need help with the kids.*

It's a scary position to be in. Expressing need and asking for help. It happens when you're used to surviving on your own.

Let Your Needs Be Known

Are you afraid to tell someone what you need? Do you feel, as I do, wary of troubling someone because you don't want to seem pitiful or you don't want to owe them because you can't reciprocate?

Jesus understands the isolation of pain. Jesus understands that when we keep it in, it separates us from the rest of the world, like damaged goods. When we let our needs be known, we open up space in our soul for friendship. We create room for the whitespace of friendship. We give ourselves a chance for someone to enter our world.

Merrianne told me she got off work at 2:00 p.m. She'd come right away. That afternoon, I cried and cried and cried. I clutched on to her, choking tears into her arms, as we stood in the middle of a playground. While Josh and Caleb played on the jungle gym, I told her what I could.

Merrianne stepped into my story. She told me she could help watch the boys next week for a few afternoons, so I could lie down and see if I could sleep.

She gave me a place in this world to be wounded. To be me.

The Isolating Message of Competence

When the panic attacks began, I stopped blogging. I didn't know if I could ever write again. Because one month in the blogosphere is like ten human years to one dog year. It's practically forever. Readers move on and you're a blip on the radar.

I knew hiding had always been my modus operandi. So I decided to take my challenge to stay present in my story and my stress into my writing world. I chose a few fellow bloggers to reach out to. I thought about how Jesus sent the disciples, two by two, out into the world.

All I need is one. I tearfully prayed.

First on my list was Holley. Holley and her friend Stephanie invited me to write with them when they first launched (in)courage at DaySpring, an online community of Christian women. Holley is as sweet as Nutella and her words spread like dessert across the page. If I was going to have a chance at crawling through this tunnel with my writing life intact, I needed another writer to collect my dog tags if I didn't make it.

"Holley . . ." I was so scared she'd ask me to leave (in)courage. Who'd want a panic-stricken woman writing on a devotional website? I'd ruin DaySpring's pretty pictures of beach houses, sunsets, and flowers with my sad tales.

"What's going on, girl?" Holley spoke from her house in Arkansas, as I pulled into a parking spot in California.

I told her about my panic attacks. I swore to her I'd never needed to step foot in a therapist's office before. I don't know how long I went on and on *about how competent I'd always been.*

"I get them too," Holley replied when I was finally done.

"What?" What was she was referring to? "You get nervous too?"

"Panic attacks," she said. "They're scary. It's hereditary for me. But, yeah, I've had 'em all my life."

Suddenly, the shame receded. I took another step into the whitespace of friendship.

134

"It's really bad. Holley, I can't even sleep. I'm afraid to go any-where anymore. I can't hardly drive. I might have to stop writing."
I held my breath. What would she say now?

"I think you're really brave, Bonnie." Holley's words weren't what I expected. "I wonder what God's doing." And with that, we talked into the hour, wondering together all the scary things that might have to happen and how we didn't know what God was doing.

"I'm really scared, Holley," my voice quivered.

"Me too," Holley said back, and she paused. "I'm always scared."

And somehow, this was funny to us. Because we snorted and started laughing between the tears.

Tell Your Story Unfinished

Do you ever find yourself waiting to get over whatever you can't seem to get over before you open up to tell your story?

Maybe like me, you've always had to make a way for yourself. It's not that you're fake or prideful. Maybe there hasn't been any safety in relationships apart from you being competent. You don't know if people will accept or reject you if they know you are bro-ken. Now that stress has you weary, you're no longer sure of who you're becoming or the new world God's having you enter into.

You may not feel competent or in control right now, but some-thing more beautiful is making its way to you: *God's story taking shape in you.*

Is letting go of competence—sharing a piece of your unfinished story—your act of faith? Make the movement to step into the free-ing, beautiful whitespace of friendship.

Friendship Frees Instead of Fixes

I wondered if I could make a new friend as anxiety-stressed me. A name began to float to my heart. *Amy.* I had just started attending a new church. We had met once, but I didn't know much about her. But I was curious. *Who is Amy? Could we be friends?*

Amy is a local missionary, working at Bayshore Christian Ministries with at-risk youth in East Palo Alto. I can't tell you why, but I felt at home with Amy. It just seemed easy to pass time together. Shoot the breeze. We both loved hiking. We'd talk about the books she was reading and her growing-up years in the Northwest, and enjoy tea while our preschoolers Caleb and Bethany worked puzzles on the floor.

Our friendship began well enough, but I decided one visit to share a traumatic memory. It didn't feel right anymore, the hiding I always did. How could our friendship grow if I swept a part of myself to the side?

Amy doesn't tell me how I should feel or what I should do. She knows getting through this journey isn't about quoting Bible verses. Amy isn't trying to fix me. She is my friend. We laugh at an electronic Winnie-the-Pooh because he sounds intoxicated when our kids play with toys powered by almost-dead batteries. We tell each other we're tired, without feeling like there's something wrong.

The whitespace of friendship. It doesn't fix us. It frees us to rest.

Do you have friends with whom you can be known without the fear of being judged? It may be time to gather your heart, put on your sandals, and pack light for the mission of friendship.

When Jesus sent the disciples into the world on a mission, he knew there were people who would not welcome them. Jesus knows rejection is part of our travels.

"Shake the dust off your feet," he told them.[1]

In other words, keep journeying until you find a home you can rest with on this roadway of faith. These homes are hearts of friends you and I can rest with. Knock on an open door. And see the face of a friend meet us.

We can welcome each other. We can sit with dust fresh on our feet. Through a phone call. An email. Face to face.

It's the whitespace of friendship. We can rest with each other awhile, as we walk into the stories God is uniquely writing in us.

We can make room for each other. As we are.

There was one friendship God began redefining to rest my soul. Except this journey didn't begin with a phone call. *This friendship was much more intimate.* This whitespace of friendship took place on a walk alone.

Pull Up a Chair—Share

What's holding you back from reaching out to find friends in your time of need?

A Whitespace Prompt—Try This

Whitespace friend list. Draw up a list of restful friends to connect with. They don't have to be your best friends and you don't have to see them frequently or for long lengths of time. Take a deep breath and start going down the list.

Pray. Ask God to give you courage to risk. Ask God to guide you. To give you intuition. To give you wisdom to find these people. They may be new people, old people, even strangers.

Ask. Keep a lookout. Listen.

Tell your story, so that they may join you and tell you theirs.

A Soul Conversation—Confide in Him

How have you been hiding your heart in relationships? Tell Jesus about the moments you felt alone in need of a friend to rest with. Ask him how you can open your heart with someone in some small, quiet way.

PART 4

whitespace signifies importance

Rest Is Intimacy

In graphic design, whitespace draws the viewer
to focus on the images and text
that are most important.
Whitespace brings an *intimacy*
and *immediacy* to the page—
awakening the foreground and
quieting the background.

13

the walk

Redefining Quiet

I need someone. I need to hold somebody close.
And I need more than this holding.

Betty Smith

Alone.

That's how I walked to school early in the mornings as a little girl, while the sun still peeked out from tree limbs, when winter skies cast long shadows from lampposts onto the sidewalk. I remember stepping over the cracks on the pavement to make time go a little faster.

I'd walk in silence as traffic buzzed by. Early commuters. I'd memorize which house came after the next, to measure how much distance was left. A white picket fence. Then the house with dusty windows sitting next to the corner unit with the front lawn of dry, yellow grass.

I remember the wood-splintered apartments covered in cobwebs bordering the neighborhood playground. I never expected anyone to join me on those long stretches of concrete and weeds between my house and school.

But one morning a man walked beside me. I was making my route through the park, where green grass grew and dew still lingered on the blades, when I saw him.

My daddy.

The Only Time

I remember being confused. My father worked as a busboy, six days a week. I didn't see him much. He worked Chinese restaurant hours, which meant I'd fallen asleep by the time he came home and he was gone when I woke in the mornings. It felt odd standing alone next to him at this hour, out here.

I stood on the sidewalk wondering, *Why are you here?* Instead I asked him, "Are you driving me to school today?"

No, he shakes his head. He tells me he wants to walk with me. He has something to tell me. "Daddy wants to live with you. But Mommy won't let me. Mommy doesn't want me here anymore. So I have to go away."

"Where are you going? Where will you live?" I look into his eyes. His lips start to quiver. His shoulders shake.

"Daddy will be . . . all by himself."

He crumples all of a sudden, pulling me to him, his body heaving and voice torn up into a thousand dry cracks. I smell his cigarettes, the ones my mom says make him stink. But to me, they smell like Daddy. And I don't want him to leave.

I cry, "Daddy. . . ." I sob and sob into my hands.

"Don't cry. Don't cry," he says.

The next thing my father does changes the course of my soul

142

the way a river cuts into rock and dirt, chiseling down into a gorge, rushing water into an echoing canyon.

He holds my hand.

As we take that long walk past the traffic light to run across a wide, busy street and turn onto a side street, my heart is breaking. The only memory I carried into my adulthood of being lovingly held by the hand is this one, when my father took mine on this walk. The only time someone reached out to tenderly touch me as a child was to tell me *he could never be with me again.*

When we finally made it to the edge of the schoolyard, he held me broken one last time. He said goodbye. Time to go to school.

Then he let go.

Whitespace of Quiet

I hate that moment.

I saw my father turn to walk away, right before I turned to walk into my classroom. He was sad and lonely. So was I.

Loneliness crept into my soul that day like a fog rolling in thick onto the highway next to the coast. I learned how to navigate well in *this fog of loneliness* for most of my life. I am comfortable with being alone. It's how I've survived heartache. It has made me strong.

After I walked home later that day, to ask my mother all the questions exploding in my head, I was told my father was a liar. That I couldn't trust anything he told me. That he was bad.

There was shouting. *Why all the questions—did I want to go live with him?* I wasn't allowed to ask questions. So I told myself I didn't need answers. But when our questions are invisible, we become invisible.

Each time I am still, they emerge: my questions.

Quietness resurfaces the thoughts and questions that are important. *Quietness connects my soulful self to Jesus.* Many times

I start my whitespace time not having anything to say. I begin my walk, ascending into the shade of redwood trees. In that quietness, my soul finally breathes. I don't have to be invisible anymore.

That's where Jesus and I meet—in the whitespace of quiet—so I can feel again.

Whatever Is Lovely

Whatever is lovely, think on these things. We often read this verse in Philippians 4:8 to mean we ought not to think of loneliness or heartbreak. But how can we live with half our souls when clearly life contains stretches of hardship and unknown transitions?

How much of life do we keep hidden from others and ourselves? How many of our true feelings do we suppress?

I used to view spending quiet time with God as a way of purging loneliness, a getting rid of questions and concerns. I would read "In repentance and rest is your salvation, in quietness and trust is your strength" (Isa. 30:15 NIV), and misunderstand *trust* to mean no more doubting.

It's become the opposite. I bring my messy self to Jesus in whitespace. Jesus wants me to trust him with *the me who surfaces when I am quiet, when I am alone.*

Each time I spend some whitespace time with Jesus, I'm allowing Jesus to hold my hand the way my daddy did when he walked me to school. God is *redefining quiet* with him through enjoying whitespace. He is uncovering desire in my soul, where there's been so much letting go.

Quiet Importance

So the next time you feel the fog of aloneness standing between you and God, make time for quiet. Don't be afraid of the cares and burdens that emerge.

Because life can only be lovely, beautiful, pure, and good—after we can bring everything that is ugly, unpleasant, messed up, and bad to the One who carries it all with us. The call to dwell on what's lovely—to take our thoughts home with the One who can guard our hearts and minds—*happens after* the apostle Paul urges us to present our deepest longings and needs to him:

Be anxious for nothing, but in everything by prayer . . . let your requests [requirements] be made known to God. (Phil. 4:6)

Quiet signifies intimacy with you is important to Jesus. Jesus is the Intimate One who cares about your burdens. Jesus loves us when we feel alone. Jesus is the companion with courage to walk with us in the quiet.

Beautiful Intimacy

He is comfortable keeping company with us in the whitespace of doubts and confusion. Jesus is capable. He knows what moves us, what can unlock us. Jesus knows how to touch us while we're stuck in the fog of stress.

Jesus does this with beauty, through nature, through music, through a text in the Word that jumps out at us or a lyric in a song, through the tears that push up through our throats or the pain inside us that dulls in the daytime but fires up at night.

Whitespace is beautiful intimacy. Just like my father met me unexpectedly on my walk that cold winter morning, *Jesus will show up somewhere along our stretch of being quiet.* I never know how he's going to touch my heart. Will he move me through something I see, a truth I discover, or beauty that surprises me?

He will meet you in a way that lets you know he is near you. He will take your hand in his.

Jesus will pull you close to his side, until you lean in close enough to hear him whisper your name and feel his heart breaking for you.

Unlike my earthly father, Jesus won't go away. Jesus will never grow tired of your stress. He'll never grow tired of you.

A Spotlight

If you give him the chance, God will tell you in new and different ways that he will be faithful. He will stay.

By redefining quiet, God is showing me he can transform my loneliest and messiest moments into the most beautiful and intimate experiences with him.

Whitespace in design identifies importance. Depending where whitespace is placed in a layout, whether in web design or an advertisement, it brings what's important to our attention, allowing the rest to fade to the sidelines. Whitespace acts like a spotlight, bringing an *intimacy* and *immediacy* to the page, awakening the foreground and quieting the background. When we enter into the whitespace of quiet, we feel the same awakening with God.

Bring Jesus closer to where you are today. What is important to your heart? Put yourself in quietness and rest in the listening heart of Jesus.

Redefine what quiet means. It isn't the absence of stress. Quiet signifies *intimate confidence in your importance* to Jesus. Allow your heart to be touched by Jesus—by choosing a moment that carries the element of quiet today. No matter how brief.

In quiet intimacy, God is reawakening rest by restoring a dream I believed was long dead.

And Jesus came to [the disciples] and *touched* them and said . . . "Do not be afraid." And lifting up their eyes, they saw no one except Jesus Himself *alone*. (Matt. 17:7–8)

Pull Up a Chair—Share

When you are stressed, are you more comfortable *being alone* rather than *being alone with God*?

What keeps you from quietness?

A Whitespace Prompt—Try This

If you're like me, longing to be awakened to rest, quietness is an element of whitespace. Quietness invites Jesus into the heart spaces, where we feel most alone.

Walk through your day. Close your eyes and picture the scenes ahead in your day. Tell Jesus what you're feeling right now as you're thinking about all that awaits you this day—what you will do, the people you will see, and the places you will be. Confide in him as friend to friend.

Choose quiet. Quiet doesn't necessarily mean being motionless. Quiet can take different forms. What types of quiet do you naturally drift toward? Do you like working with your hands as you knit, garden, or craft, or do you like moving your body by taking a walk or bicycling? Or do you gravitate to quiet when there is music or you are engaged in art?

Quietness is fluid. Being still doesn't need to happen at the same time, doing the same thing, every day. It can happen at a bench outside a café, pausing to take a picture, or getting lost focusing on something you enjoy, like reading a book.

Quietness in pauses. Quietness happens when we are in transit too: driving in our car, waiting at the doctor's office, biking to school, or stepping into a hot shower before bed. Think through your day and zero in on the moments you are alone. Prompt yourself to imagine Jesus quietly keeping you company, listening to you—*because he is*. He is in you.

A Soul Conversation—Confide in Him

What is your first memory of really being held in intimate quiet?

14

the hallway

Restoring Creativity

Every artist dips his brush in his own soul.

Henry Ward Beecher

She stood there.

Tall. Athletic. Tan and smiling. She had dark hair. So did I.

Her eyes shone bright and clear. She was the kind of girl you'd want for a babysitter.

She carried a notebook in one arm, a bag of books slung on the other, as she waved hello at the door.

"Hi! I'm Laura." She beamed a smile. She was seventeen.

We had only spoken on the phone and I was meeting her for the first time. Eric and I needed a new babysitter for date nights and our church's high school pastor had recommended Laura.

After coming home that evening, I sat on the living room floor with her, waiting for her dad to pick her up.

"So, how's this year going? Junior year is big . . . college and stuff," I commented.

"Yeah. I'm applying," she answered.

"Do you know what you want to study—where you'd like to go?"

Laura took a huge breath and exhaled her answer.

"Writing." She sounded tentative. "I want to be a writer." She shrugged her shoulders and played with her fingers.

"That's awesome." I asked her to tell me more.

Laura wanted to write fantasy. Her words bubbled with excitement. She didn't know if her stories would ever get published, but she said she'd be happy as long as she writes.

"You're already a writer, you know that?" I queried.

"Well . . . we'll see." Her voice trailed. "I don't know if that's *really* what God wants me to do." Her smile faded and her face turned quiet.

"Laura. Being a writer—it's not what you do." I held her gaze to make sure my words landed. "It's *who you are*. It's who God made you inside."

Laura's eyes began to water. "That's beautiful," she said. Laura didn't know it, but I've been stuck inside the house the entire week unable to write, simply trying to breathe through my panic attacks. But I saw her. There is a recognition.

I saw the seventeen-year-old in me.

Seventeen

That night, after kissing Eric goodnight, I took my nightly post of insomnia. One o'clock. Two o'clock. Three. As I started drifting off at last, it happened. A memory triggered by meeting Laura.

The hallway. I'm standing there in the dark. I'm seventeen.

My momma shut her bedroom door in my face. She locked it, so I couldn't come in. I hear sliding closet doors being slammed around, drawers opening and thumping shut. She's raging.

And I'm shaking. I don't know what to do. I'm biting into one of the college brochures I'm hugging, trying to cry silently. If I cry too loudly, she'll hear me. The bedroom door will fly open and it'll be worse.

I couldn't get this memory out of my mind. Even as I went about my tasks the next day, my body could not leave the hallway. Panic attacks wracked me, subsided, and resumed over the next forty-eight hours until I went in to see Dr. P.

The Most Natural Thing

I had been plotting my escape for years. Getting the As. Taking AP classes and checking the extracurricular box, joining French Club at lunch hour, competing in speech and debate, and playing zero period orchestra. Anything that didn't cost money or require after-school involvement. I had to be home after school to take care of my little sister.

I had to be home because Momma said so. I was imprisoned by my life. College was my ticket out.

I'd always loved writing. It came easy for me. It was the one thing in my life no one could take away from me.

I didn't have to be good at it. I didn't have to think about it. Writing was just what I did. It's the most natural thing I could do.

The little girl in me is a writer.

No Plans

My mom didn't speak English, couldn't read. She dropped out of school when she was thirteen, growing up in Hong Kong. She said she had to stay home and take care of her five younger siblings. She didn't talk to me about college. So I never really thought about it. Until freshman year in high school.

Mr. O'Neal ran a summer job program at a computer lab at Foothill College for kids from low-income families. One day as I was formatting floppy discs, he asked me about college. *Not sure*, I told him. I needed to get a job and take care of my mom and sister.

"You are going to college, Miss Bonnie." Mr. O'Neal, six feet tall, sat like a gentle giant at his desk. "I want you applying for Ivy League schools. Don't stay. Leave."

Was it possible? I spent hours in the career counselor's office and began collecting my brochures. I set my sights on the East Coast. I wanted to go far away and make my life in a world inhabited by story—created by journalists, authors, poets, musicians, and literary professors. Freedom.

Looking back at that seventeen-year-old me, I wish she hadn't told her momma her plans. I wish she had just gone east.

The Wrong People

It didn't feel honest mailing out college applications without telling her. I didn't think she had reason to object. It wouldn't cost her any money. I waited until after dinner, after I did the dishes.

"I'm gonna apply for college, Momma. I might go to the East Coast," I told her. I opened up the college brochures and showed her how beautiful the campuses were.

She sat there silent on the living room couch that pilled like an old acrylic sweater.

"I'm really good, Momma," I proceeded with measured caution. "My English teachers all say I'm really good. And Mr. O'Neal says I can get in."

"Of course they say you're good," Momma's face was ashen. "They're teachers, what do you expect. Mr. O'Neal? He runs that program for poor kids. I'm sure he told you that."

"I've talked to the college recruiters. They say I've got a good chance," I countered. But I suddenly didn't feel so sure anymore.

Momma started shaking her head at me, like I'm some dumb girl who got suckered into something stupid. "Those schools are for rich kids, families who have money. Not you." She said it to me the way a mother tells her daughter about the ABCs.

I told her I had it all worked out. Grants, scholarships, and money from the summer and part-time work.

"If you go, who will take care of me? And your sister?" She started getting upset. "You've forgotten who you are. You are my daughter. Now you wanna leave me?"

I pleaded with her. Then she said the words that have haunted my soul since.

"You've been listening to the wrong people, Bonnie." She stood up now, her scorn gathering strength over me.

Like an animal snared in a coil-spring trap, the spine of my heart breaks in half. I have no more words. I can't hear the voices of my teachers, Mr. O'Neal or anybody. The world filled with books and beautiful stories suddenly felt stupid and unreal.

"You . . . a writer? I know you. You're just selfish. You want to fly away, now that you have wings. You weren't so high and mighty when you were small and needy. Now you want to have the good life without me?" The words slayed me with a thousand cuts. I broke down sobbing, begging her to stop.

"If you leave, you're on your own." My mother drew a line in the sand. "Don't ever call me Momma again." Her words cursed the air. "You'll be pitiful. Because everyone will have family. Except you."

She slammed the door in front of me as I followed behind. The brochures in my hands no longer shined glossy and new. They felt wrong. This other beautiful life was not for me.

As I stood there blinded by tears, I saw my sister through the doorway into our room, lying on the bed.

It's too late for me, I thought. *But it's not too late for her. I can make money. Take care of my mother and give my sister the chance to choose.*

It calmed my heart. I made my decision.

I'd stay nearby. I'd enroll at UCLA to become a computer engineer.

I turned around in the hallway, walked into the kitchen and shoved my college brochures down—past the empty milk carton, leftover dinner scraps, and junk mail—into the garbage can.

I chose to kill the dream. Of who God made me to be.

Creative Whitespace

Conflicted. This is a place of torture. Indecision. Where you don't feel at peace with who you are, what you feel, and what you want. It's where I often find myself feeling guilty for taking time out for me.

I feel selfish for choosing whitespace for me. It's easier to ignore that desire, to do and be what others need.

I often say, "All I want is Jesus." But I forget Jesus wants the me he imprinted with a unique personality and heartfelt desires. I had shoved my dreams down so many times that nurturing my soul wasn't important anymore. It was much safer to be functional than emotionally engaged.

Do you ever find this dynamic at play in you too? When you crave *creative whitespace*—to enjoy what feeds your soul—do you shrink back because it feels like a waste of time?

When we brush ourselves to the side and say, "It's not important," what we're really saying is, "*I'm* not important."

Spiritual whitespace dares us to say, "I *am* important." Even if we can only manage saying it in a reticent whisper.

The Artistic You

Just as whitespace attracts the eye to an important object by creating restful boundaries, spiritual whitespace moves our hearts front and center with God. *Spiritual whitespace brings one thing into focus: the God-sized dream in you.*[1] It's the kind of dream my friend Holley says "begins in God's heart that he places in yours."

When we live without space for those dreams, we become numb. It isn't really living. It's called *survival*.

Because when you lose hope for yourself, it is easy to give yourself and your life away to others, where putting priority on yourself feels self-centered. We neglect our soul. We separate ourselves from the artist in us.

Do you ever find yourself thinking about her—*the artistic you?* God does. He whispers, *I see you. I made you. I love you.*

When you get closer to what truly moves your heart, you will touch the places that are still tender. It's there—in those private places of freedom where you meet with God—your creative self speaks.

Even if critical voices threaten to empty us, Jesus sees.

It reminds me of Jesus sitting at the water's edge.

Out of the Corner

The Scriptures tell us crowds were pressing in on Jesus. Then

> [Jesus] noticed two empty boats at the water's edge, for the fishermen had left them and were washing their nets. (Luke 5:2 NLT)

With crowds pushing in to meet him, you wouldn't think Jesus would notice something as insignificant as empty boats. But he did.

Jesus noticed

two empty boats
at the water's edge.

Jesus noticed this out of the corner of his eye. *Because he saw the fishermen.* Washing their nets.

The fishermen were done.

They had fished all night. Exhausted and worn.

155

And there was nothing to show for any of it.

Then Jesus did the most amazing thing. Jesus got into one of the boats.

Jesus climbed into an empty boat.

What have you left? Is Jesus calling you back?

An Empty Boat

During my therapy session, the shock of seeing it all again horrified me. I felt angry. *Why are you doing this, God? What's the point—showing me a dream that already died?* As Jesus stood facing me in the scene, I looked into his eyes. They were sad and full of tears.

Jesus began showing me something he held in his hands. They were the brochures, tattered and soiled. He had fished them out of the garbage.

I remember, it seemed he was saying. *My dreams for you. It broke my heart, seeing yours break at seventeen.*

Deep Waters

As I bitterly cried, I remembered what Jesus said to Peter:

Put out into the deep water, and let down your nets for a catch. (v. 4)

Where are your deep waters, friend? Are you empty of dreams? Behind every pain lies a lost dream. Perhaps, like me, you've made a choice at some point to forget. You've tried to shield yourself from that loss by submerging your dreams.

It's too late, you tell yourself. *It's been too long. Another lifetime ago.*

You've moved on and gained strength by helping others.

But Jesus sees the nets you've left. Jesus sees how you've washed them clean and dragged your boat back onto the shore.

156

He feels the ache inside that comes from having no catch. He knows your soul has grown hungry. He sees you are too tired to go back out.

Yet Jesus stands on the shore at the break of dawn. He calls to you and me—

"Cast the net on the [other] side of the boat and you will find a catch" (John 21:6).

Jesus sees the empty nets.

Put out where it is deeper and let down your nets.

It's not too late. To come as you are.

Not Too Late

Remember the dreams he's placed in you. Take the time to go where the water runs deep. Go where you don't usually wander.

Wade where Jesus is still creating in you. Choose creative whitespace.

Choose to feel and seek beauty. Travel to distant lands of discovery—art, music, writing, painting, photography, baking, cooking, gardening, decorating, script writing, singing, beading, sewing, crafting—whatever moves you closer to who God made you.

It's not too late to rest in creative whitespace.

You are the creative imprint of your heavenly Father. You are like him and he is like you.

God rests, not because it's a rule. God rests because he loves making beautiful things. He loves making them come alive *through you at rest.*

Jesus wants to meet you in the intimate whitespace of restoring creativity.

Sometimes we can guard our hearts so capably and well it takes the tenderness of pain to awaken them back to life. So they can say yes to God again and let him back in.

This touch was needed in my prayer life. I needed a new intimacy there too.

> Fan into flame the gift of God, which is in you . . . for God gave us a spirit not of fear but of power and love and self-control. (2 Tim. 1:6–7 ESV)

Pull Up a Chair—Share

What have you left? What is your empty boat?

How is God calling you back?

A Whitespace Prompt—Try This

Find your creative whitespace. When you were a little girl, what did you enjoy doing? What came naturally to you?

Enjoy God in inspiring places. Where are places that inspire the artistic you? Outdoors near the beach or mountains? Indoors in front of an easel or a desk? Maybe it's experiential, clicking behind a camera lens, walking through an art gallery, listening to live music, or observing life from a chair at a café? Is it through learning, taking a class you've always wanted to explore?

A Soul Conversation—Confide in Him

Is there a God-sized dream you left in the hallway of your life?

How did you make the decision—whose voice did you listen to? Share any angry or hurtful feelings with God. Confide in him.

15

alone with you

Redefining Prayer

Touch has a memory.

John Keats

He kissed me.

Under the gentle breeze blowing through the swaying limbs of a willow tree, Eric wrapped his arms around my waist.

I was standing up on the curb, but even then, the top of my head only reached his chin. I was snuggled in close. Resting. Leaning in until my shoulders softened, I could feel his shirt smooth against my cheek. I felt like the petal of a cherry blossom, blown in from spring rain falling quietly at night, sticking wet against the window pane, right before dawn casts the warmth of its first light into an empty room.

Without a word, he relaxed his hold, and I felt his cheek nestling down to mine.

And still without one word, I felt how very close his breath was to mine.

It was our first kiss.

And the ones we took next were with each other, with tenderness, speaking from our hearts. In that one moment, he who would eventually become my husband and I stepped into a place inside us that is both as young as it is old, new as it is familiar and worn.

It's a feeling and a knowing that we both found something in being with each other we could not find with anyone else.

That place is called home.

Your Soul's Home

Home. It's where prayer takes us to Jesus. Where it's just me and Jesus.

Even if there isn't a word spoken between us, praying in whitespace allows me to explore where my soul feels most at home to enjoy time with Jesus.

Praying in whitespace is finding ways to open my heart. Without the pressure of speaking a word. To engage my senses. So I can feel his presence. So that my soul can once again feel. See. Touch. Hear.

And then, only then, can I receive.

Jesus knows this. That is why he wants to meet us in the secret places within us.

This is where our soul speaks with him.

In spiritual whitespace, we step away from everyone else. It's the place inside us where we listen to music that reminds us of a special time, when we look at a photograph and remember how very happy or sad we felt in that moment.

It's the innermost being the psalmist references, where we find pieces of ourselves flicker in a story being told on the silver screen or in between pages of a book.

You desire truth in the innermost being. (Ps. 51:6)

160

Prayer, after all, is being truthful with God about what we think, feel, need, and want.

It's giving God a chance to let himself in. For us to miss him and wish he were here in front of us.

Sometimes, with the many roles and functions we perform at work, at school, at home, with friends, and even at church, we don't give ourselves a chance to spend time with God from that innermost place.

When we imagine making space and time to be alone with Jesus, we can become overwhelmed by words.

What would I say? How should I pray?

Often when I'm working through my stress or wrestling with my worries, I don't feel like praying. I can hardly understand myself and I don't have peace. How can I talk to God in this state?

This is when I'm the most tempted to just hide away and wait until I'm better. That's how I end up staying away from him.

Without One Word

I've learned that times of confusion—when the rush of too many words or lack of words stifles my desire—are times I have a chance to take a risk. To be intimate with Jesus by allowing him into my world. Rather than thinking how can I be with Jesus, I ask myself, *How can I let Jesus be with me?*

Prayer doesn't always need to be a verbal conversation for a set amount of time that happens at a specific place.

When I have absolutely nothing to say to him, will I let him spend time with me—where I want to be?

Can Jesus really make his home in me?

This is where I have learned to rest and pray by simply being with Jesus, as I am.

Without one word.

Hunger and Need

This is what Jesus was trying to say a long time ago, to people who had lost touch with the nearness of God. People had somehow found such safety in doing Sabbath that they forgot how intimate God wanted things to be between us from the very beginning.

They were so good at doing what they thought God wanted them to do, they missed out on how much God wanted to be with them. *They were doing rest to draw closer to God, rather than enjoying rest because God was present with them.*

One of the ways the Bible comes alive for me is to imagine myself in the story. I entered into the scene that day Jesus was taking a walk in a field with his disciples. It was a day set aside for no activity, to honor God on the Sabbath day.

> [Jesus] was passing through the grainfields on the Sabbath, and His disciples began . . . picking the heads of grain. The Pharisees were saying to Him, "Look, why are they doing what is not lawful on the Sabbath?" And He said to them, "Have you never read what David did *when he was in need* and he and his companions became hungry; how he entered the house of God . . . and ate the consecrated bread, which is not lawful for anyone to eat?" . . . Jesus said to them, *"The Sabbath was made for man, and not man for the Sabbath."* (Mark 2:23–27)

Jesus and the disciples were doing something as ordinary as picking wheat from the fields they were walking through. Where were they going? And what were they doing together?

I saw Jesus leading the conversation away from what God required (Sabbath laws) to how David felt in need (soul rest). Jesus talked about hunger. Just as Jesus taught the disciples a better way, Jesus desires to step into our world.

Jesus wants to give rest that works for us.

162

A Taste of Honey

"The Sabbath was made for man, and not man for the Sabbath" (v. 27). I read this over and over again. This verse began to blossom, like a bud suddenly released to open its first petal. Ever so slightly.

It's often said we were made for rest. But Jesus says the opposite. He tells me that *rest was made for me.*

As I thought more deeply about this—like the taste of honey finally surfacing on your tongue with a slow sip of tea—I understood what Jesus was saying. He was moving me away from spending time with him as a response to a command. Instead, Jesus was turning my heart to rest in his gaze—as a response to his invitation. To open my heart and let him in.

> *Bonnie, I know you feel needy.*
> *What is it that you're hungering for?*
> *What do you find refreshing, sad, lonely, comforting, or beautiful?*
> *Let me spend time. With you. This way.*

This might be how things began in that first whitespace when God walked with Adam and Eve in the Garden of Eden. When he created man and woman to walk this earth in their bare skin, he walked with them under the cool of the trees. He talked about the dusk he was painting later that evening, while Adam and Eve enjoyed the honey scent of sweet fruit trees lightly blowing in through the grass, brought by the north winds.

Conversing with Jesus

Jesus is Sabbath to us today. We are no longer limited by where we are or what we are doing in order to enjoy *a soul conversation* with him. We can engage our hearts, bodies, minds, thoughts, and emotions to be with him. *We are the new Garden of Eden.* It's God in us today.

> So there remains a Sabbath rest for the people of God. For the one who has entered His rest has himself also rested from his works, as God did from His. (Heb. 4:9–10)

Whitespace in art directs a viewer's eye to what's important. It acts as a border, separating unrelated elements from what's central. It makes the art beautiful. Spiritual whitespace does the same. Spiritual whitespace reminds us God's presence is what's important. It redefines what it means to pray with God.

In the next two chapters, I'd like to share how God is redefining prayer for me. Let's take a second look at what it means to have *a soul conversation*—to open up our world, to let Jesus in.

It's like that journey I took to stand on the curb, to lean myself into Eric's embrace.

That is what praying in whitespace looks like.

It's reorienting our hearts and our bodies to be in a place to receive. To give Jesus access.

Just like a first kiss, we can take the risk. The time. *To put ourselves out in a place where that moment can happen.*

Where we can be still enough.

To be touched.

To be reached.

And to lean in close enough to hear a whisper.

Feel a movement.

To look into Jesus's gaze.

And maybe, just maybe. That moment will come. *Then prayer will be more than just words.*

It will be savoring his presence and realizing Jesus wants to be with us.

Not because we should be with him. Not because we are doing Sabbath because he commands it. Not because we must spend time with him or else bad things will happen.

We are there because we want to be touched in a way that reminds us we are home.

We are loved.

We are someone worth spending time with.

Pull Up a Chair—Share

How is God redefining prayer time with you?

Have you somehow, like me, separated restful activities from "spiritual experiences" of being with Jesus? Have you defined resting with God to look a certain way?

A Whitespace Prompt—Try This

Reminisce. Think back to times when praying felt intimate and personal, when God felt close to you. What elements moved you?

Where were you?

How were you feeling?

What were you doing?

What time of day was it?

Use these questions to spark the next whitespace you take with Jesus and incorporate one element.

A Soul Conversation—Confide in Him

What are the pressures you feel about spending "alone time" with God to pray? Tell him what they are. Jesus understands. He wants to draw near.

16

a love note

Redefining Time in God's Word

Let your religion be less of a theory and more
of a love affair.

G. K. Chesterton

I remember the first time I got an email from Eric. I read it over
and over. It wasn't more than a few lines.

How are you? It was nice to talk to you.

I remembered the shape of the paragraph, how the sentences
wrapped around at the return of a line. Even though I couldn't
hear his voice, his words placed a conversation in a quiet corner
of my heart. I couldn't see him, but he felt near.

The digital letters Eric sent my way collected like beads of morning dew on clover. They didn't need to be many to make my heart
happy. His words stayed with me.

It was a love note.

Do you remember your first love note—how it kept you company throughout the day, even as you worked? How you could trace every letter, recalling every I and T? You never got tired reading the same words.

It didn't matter how much time separated the two of you. Traffic, meetings, and chores in between. Time apart only meant there was so much more to talk about later. You picked up right where you left off. Sometimes all you could do was leave a voice mail or send a quick text. In the end, every communication is intimately beautiful and good.

When we think about spending time with God, we often beat ourselves up for not spending enough time. That guilt kills intimacy of the heart. Whitespace doesn't keep track of the amount of time. Time doesn't exist in whitespace.

Spiritual whitespace takes place in the eternity of our hearts.

He has made everything beautiful in its time. He has also set eternity in the human heart; yet no one can fathom what God has done from beginning to end. (Eccles. 3:11 NIV)

Eternity can be experienced in just one word God sets on your heart. Just like a love note, one word can transport us to the nearness of God. His words keep us company and tell us we are remembered. We are a part of his heart.

Spiritual whitespace is created in our soul whenever we fill it with a love note. From God.

What is that one word God's placed on your heart today—this week—or this year?

One Word

Sometimes we put so much pressure on ourselves to hear God say something new. But there are seasons where one word is more than enough. Sometimes one word trickles into a series of soul conversations and takes us on a weeklong, monthlong, or yearlong journey to savor, cry over, and explore with Jesus.

Time is no longer measured in the number of words we receive from God, but in the intimacy of being understood.

Is the word from a message you heard on Sunday? Or maybe a quote from a book on your nightstand?

A word from God doesn't have to come from a memory verse from Scripture.

It can be a lyric from a new song.

It can be visual. Something you see. Take a picture.

Is it an image that's floating in your thoughts? Sketch it.

Is it poetry or a riff from a jazz standard you just heard on the radio?

Or is it the push of water on your skin in a quiet pool on a summer morning as you swim?

What speaks to your heart?

A Living Voice

Jesus invites us to engage our senses. He isn't limited by time. He speaks to us where we are. His words don't always have to come from the pages of our Bible (although they most often do). The author of Hebrews tells us:

> Let us, therefore, *make every effort* to enter that rest. . . . For the *word of God is alive and active*. . . . It penetrates even to dividing soul and spirit . . . it judges the thoughts and attitudes of the heart. (Heb. 4:11–12 NIV)

The "word of God" used here is the Greek word *logos*—translated as *living voice*. This means God is not limited to the written word.

God uses *everything living* to speak into our lives. He knows what's on your heart and the everyday life you are living. God leaves us love notes in that everyday life to let us know: he is a part of our living story.

Logos. It's another word used to mean *story*.

Story is how John describes Jesus as the Word that became flesh two thousand years ago. And today, Jesus's story continues to take on flesh in you and me.

Jesus is telling his story—alive and new—through each of our voices, individual interests, and passions. That's how he speaks to us, through the things that move our hearts.

Refreshing Your Soul

God's word is *living*, translated from the Greek word *zao*. Zao means *fresh*. Soul conversation with God happens when we refresh our souls. What awakens your soul? What refreshes you?

The love notes God sends us are also *active*. Those sparks— moments we are touched—can happen any time. Spending time immersed in things that move us, whether films, books, art, decorating, journaling, or nature, injects energy and new ideas into our conversations with God.

Many times, we tell ourselves quiet time with God must happen at the same time, for a specific duration, and at the same place in order for it "to count."

Yet Jesus whispers—

Don't worry how long we have. A moment is forever in eternity.

Let me send you a word. In ways that speak to you. Ways that prompt your heart.

To let you know.

I'm thinking of you. I love you. I am at home in you.

We can redefine what it means to spend time with Jesus. Times with Jesus are moments we enjoy with him. A word. A Scripture.

170

A picture. A song. A new recipe. Moving colors through yarn and hook. Cutting fabric or paper as you craft.

Refreshing your soul with Jesus is whitespace.

Intimacy, Not Balance Sheets

Are you disturbed by how stress has cut your day into pieces that can't seem to stay together long enough for "quiet time"? Jesus stands in those shards with us. We can rest with him outside the constraints of time. *Your heart is his throne.*

> We have this hope as an anchor for the soul, firm and secure. It enters the inner sanctuary behind the curtain where our forerunner, Jesus, has entered on our behalf. (Heb. 6:19–20 NIV)

In the same way Jesus entered the temple, we are the living sanctuaries of God's presence. We are God's dwelling place. Jesus meets with us in this inner whitespace residing within us: spiritual whitespace.

True spiritual rest is no longer limited by time or place. Because eternity now dwells in us, and because we carry his presence in us, we can enter into rest whenever. However. As is.

Jesus has entered and he is staying. Our souls are his sanctuary.

This realization redefined for me what it means to spend time with Jesus. *It's taken away the balance sheet between me and him.* It's more about the intimacy of being together, because we're mindful of each other.

As I focus on awakening my heart with Jesus, something beautiful happens. I develop a deepening desire *for more*. I become more creative about how to steal time away together. To confide in each other. And plan for longer stretches of conversation.

Give yourself permission to try different ways to enjoy Jesus's company. Be alone with him. As you do, Jesus will do something new.

171

Jesus is reminding me why I'd want to steal a private moment with him. He brought me back to a crowded room one night where I wanted to fall in love. He wanted me to think back on sweetness, poetry and songs I'd long abandoned. I had forgotten what it felt like to hear my name whispered. Jesus began redefining solitude for me.

Pull Up a Chair—Share

How is God speaking to you in everyday life, apart from the written word in Scripture?

How would taking away the balance sheet between you and God affect your time with him? How would you refresh your soul?

A Whitespace Prompt—Try This

My favorite things. What are your favorite things lately—flowers, a song, a color theme, a movie, a Bible verse, a quote, a poem, a book, or a memento? Connect your heart to God by placing these things in your week to prompt you of his presence. Enjoy them, mindful he's enjoying them with you.

One-word whitespace. What is one word on your heart lately?

Capture God's love notes in everyday life. Be on the lookout for things, conversations, or experiences to cross your path that remind you of God's One Word for you.

Capture God's love notes through your senses. They can be audio, visual, experiential, or written.

Create a one-word collage. Do it visually with post-its, frame it, take photos; do it online on Instagram, Evernote, Pinterest, or a blog; log it in your journal; or design it as décor in your room.

One-word study. Pop the word in an online Scripture concordance and look up verses that contain that one word. Allow that word to trickle into a quiet stream of whitespace.

Resist the urge to put a time constraint on this soul conversation. Savor your One Word.

A Soul Conversation—Confide in Him

God's love note to you. If God wrote a love note to you today, what would it say? Write it down. Begin with "Dear (your name)" and allow that note from God to you to be written through your hand, as the Holy Spirit speaks through you.

An As-Is letter from you. If you wrote a letter to God today, what would it say? Write him that letter now. Not as you want to be or wish to be. As is.

17

solitude

Redefining Place

Only a house quiet as snow, a space for myself
to go, clean as paper before the poem.

Sandra Cisneros

I wanted to steal a moment alone with him at the singles ministry
potluck social on Friday night. We had been emailing back and
forth for a couple weeks since he first visited the group, walking
in tall and quiet. I wanted to get close and feel what it was like to
look into his eyes.

I was waiting for my chance. I wanted to enjoy a conversation
where something from his heart might slip through—a thought
just between us two. The house was packed, people buzzing by,
pressing in, how-are-you chats in small groups collecting. Nooks
and crannies got filled, and it seemed he was always over there,
with me always here with someone next to me.

There is a time and place for group activity and sharing, but sometimes you want to feel special. *You want a private moment.*

I've thought a lot about all the solitude I've been forced by anxiety to experience. It just can't be that good, falling apart all alone. But sometimes, solitude is the only place you can go to feel safe enough to fall apart.

You wouldn't think these painful times would lead me back to something so lovey-dovey-gooey as my first days falling in love with Eric. But they have. I ask myself how this heart of mine that has tasted the sweetness of falling in love can be so heartsick and choke with such darkness and fear. It scares me, these two different hearts beating inside.

Dr. P tells me this is perfectly normal. It turns out you and I can live in two places when we are overwhelmed by stress. When I'm "processing a memory"—reliving a traumatic scene in my life— Dr. P invites Jesus to enter the scene with me. He asks me to replay it, with Jesus there.

It's there, in the middle of my torment, that I often hear just one word.

It's one word Jesus whispers. It's completely jarring, like the spinning top in the movie *Inception*. It's a totem—a small personal object—that lets the dreamer know whether he is dreaming or awake. If what he is experiencing is real.

The word Jesus whispers—that brings rest and safety back to my heart—is *my name*.

Your Name

Your name. It's what Mary heard alone in the garden at the tomb. Jesus said her name. And she recognized him, even in her stress and turmoil. When she heard Jesus say her name, she wasn't alone anymore.

Her time spent in despairing solitude brought her Jesus.

How does Jesus say your name? When was the last time you heard him speak it?

So much is in a name. It reminds me of the first time Eric and I embraced, when he whispered "Bonnie." It brings me back to the first time my children said "Mommy." The first moments when each of my babies broke out of me—when the doctor placed their bodies warm and alive against my chest, I looked into their eyes, soothed their cheeks with my fingers, and cradled them in my arms.

I whispered their names.

Josh.

Caleb.

I knew they couldn't see me. But I knew they would hear my voice. And I hoped their heartbeats would rest a little slower, knowing I was near. I would be their comfort in a world they had battled to enter.

It's been the same way hearing God during my year of panic attacks. I can't see him in ways I used to. I've been so overwhelmed with physical distress I can't even focus or read. And yet, when I look out onto the wave of an ocean, brush past yellow blossoms of a wildflower, or feel rain lightly fall along a trail, I hear God whispering my name.

Poiema

Solitude has redefined my place of whitespace.

Whitespace used to mainly happen at my desk in front of a Bible, reading through Scripture with a fine-tooth comb. But I've now come to discover solitude can lead me deeper into my heart—in places beyond my desk.

Arthur Rubenstein, one of the greatest pianists of the twentieth century, when asked how he creates the tone he plays, said he once heard a woman sing.[1] She sang with the most beautiful tone and he observed how she would pause. *She stopped to take a breath.* Rubenstein learned to do the same at the piano. Every time his fingers paused to touch the keys, it was like taking a breath.

The act of pausing at the keys created a beautiful tone. Rubenstein said when he touched the keys, he would *feel the song sing* in him. Touching the keys made him feel the emotion. Rubenstein confessed many young people could play the piano perfectly, technically much better than him. But then he would ask the young person, "When will you start making music? When will you become an artist?"

Arthur Rubenstein's words moved me deeply. *Was my heart the same for the fingers of God?* When I stood there alone on a summer-scorched hill, as the wind brushed through boughs waving in the breeze, were those his fingertips pausing right where it was lonely and aching within me?

Were my dreams, longings, and brokenness all part of a song God was singing in me? What would emerge from my life if I paused long enough to let his Spirit breathe? Isn't that who God is after all—an artist?

With trembling lips, I knew my heart found it all too difficult to believe I could be anything of a song. My life felt more like a broken melody.

God gently said, *You are. My song.*

For we are God's workmanship, created in Christ Jesus to do good works, which God prepared in advance for us to do. (Eph. 2:10 NIV 1984)

The root word for workmanship is *poiema*. It means "work of art." *Poiema* gives us the English word *poem*. You and I are God's poetry. We are his masterpiece.

When we pause in solitude, a beautiful tone is created. God touching our soul is God's workmanship. We are God's artwork.

Soul Art

Poiema has irrevocably transformed how I view solitude—alone time—with God. The artist Pablo Picasso said, "Without great solitude, no serious work is possible."[2] *Poeima* has redefined *where* I spend time with God. My conversations with him are no longer limited to the discipline of Bible study or reciting memory verses.

My focus has turned to seeking out places where my heart wakes up to God's creative expression. Solitude no longer means ticking off coursework as a follower of Christ, like prerequisites in the school of faith. *Solitude has become the canvas of whitespace I can enter into—vibrant and real—for God.* I want that special tone to resonate from my soul. I want a quality in my relationship with Jesus that only comes through breathing in whitespace.

Solitude has become my soul art. It's an intriguing spiritual journey: How can I encourage myself to stop long enough—to pause in solitude—to feel God's emotions in me?

Soulful solitude is changing how I relate to others too. I'm connecting with people's stories more deeply. I find myself freer to listen. Instead of trying to figure out what to say or how to help them, I offer a space for others. Together, we can pause.

And in listening to each other, we can be that breath for Christ. We allow the Holy Spirit to comfort, touch, and recognize God's story in each of us. We can testify: *God has a song in you.* In the very moments we feel weak, God's song of love and faithfulness is singing over each of us:

> He will take great delight in you, he will quiet you with his love, he will rejoice over you with singing. (Zeph. 3:17 NIV 1984)

If Words Aren't Needed

There is a time and place to study Scripture intellectually. But doing so is not a magic wand to avoid the hard places. Solitude reminds us we were made for beautiful things. Even when they break.

We often struggle with how we ought to pray. What we should ask for or say. But what if audible words aren't needed for prayer? Because, you see, those moments of silence are simply beautiful moments Jesus is praying for us:

> Because Jesus lives forever, he has a permanent priesthood. Therefore he is able to save completely . . . because *he always lives to intercede for* [*us*]. (Heb. 7:24–25 NIV)

If you knew Jesus was praying for you—that he's got your worries covered—where would you go to relax and find beauty? Allowing yourself to enjoy those places while Jesus intercedes on your behalf becomes an act of faith.

Prayer can even be found in the fragrance of flowers, a place in your home where you pause in your day to enjoy them. Places of beauty can remind us Jesus is praying for us. Incense, after all, is how prayers look in heaven.[3]

A Living Prayer

Prayer is listening, like an intimate conversation between two people who are alone at last. Silence reminds us words aren't required to be loved by God.

> In the same way, the Spirit helps us in our weakness. We do not know what we ought to pray for, but the Spirit himself intercedes for us through wordless groans. (Rom. 8:26 NIV)

Teach us to pray, the disciples asked. Jesus taught them by praying with them and for them everywhere: in storms, hiding in upper room secrecy, in front of dead men, with blind beggars, and in a dark garden of tears. They *experienced* prayer.

Jesus was the living prayer.

And so are we, temples lit within by the same Flame, the Holy Spirit, dwelling in us.[4]

Jesus in us.
Living prayers.
No matter where you are. That's who you are. You and me.

Pull Up a Chair—Share

What are ways you can enjoy solitude in a soulful way with God?

How can you nurture your soul as God's *poeima*—his work of art in you?

A Whitespace Prompt—Try This

What is Jesus praying for me right now? Write the prayer you imagine Jesus is praying for you right now. Asking this question takes us away from worrying about how to pray. Simply reflect how Jesus is thinking of you.

How is God whispering my name today? Engage your senses. Be on the lookout for the ways Jesus is letting you know you are on his mind.

A Soul Conversation—Confide in Him

When was the first time you heard someone whisper your name tenderly?

18

the wild things

Beauty and Mystery

> You ache with it all; and the more mysterious it
> is, the more you ache.
>
> Fyodor Dostoevsky

I fled to the bathroom. Shut the door and locked it tight.

I didn't dare run. Or else she might chase me down. My mother was livid. How selfish and cheap I was to go on a road trip with my friends and the guy I liked during the holiday weekend, leaving her all alone at home.

She threw my closet open, yanking my clothes off hangers, and ripped the seams apart. *You've forgotten who you belong to. Without me, you'd be nothing. Everything you have is mine.*

She stormed out of the room and came back with shears. The sound of fabric rending and the bullets of ugly words flying tore into my soul.

Just this one plank of wood separates us, I thought, as my mother yelled and pounded against the door.

This was how it always happened. I'd say something she didn't like. Do something that wasn't right.

I would escape to the bathroom and look at myself in the mirror. I looked at my hair, the curve of eyebrows in need of plucking, the pupils in my eyes, or my chin. I'd stare into the mirror and cry.

Somewhere in that mirror, I couldn't hear her anymore. I'd start thinking about other things. I felt calm. I was all right. But I wasn't.

I only wanted to disappear. From what was happening. From what was wrong. I stopped feeling. My panic. My sadness.

I felt strong. But really I was numb.

Constant, Frenetic Stress

I think we disappear in more grown-up ways. We each have our own ways of numbing.

Being busy. Designing a photoshopped life.

Disappearing into Google searches, overdosing on a digital life.

Pleasing others. Playing a role.

Working hard to make a place for ourselves in this world.

Constantly searching for the next finish line.

We scour the landscape of our lives and seek the face of a rocky mountain in the distance to scale. Where we are now today is not where we want to be.

It's wearying. This constant, frenetic stress to keep moving. Perhaps you find yourself fighting these thoughts as I do:

I'm not enough for my children, my husband, or my friends.

My home could be more lovely.

I should have more friends.

I am afraid to stop. I don't want to be nothing. I don't want to feel the wilderness that is my soul. I cannot subdue my restless heart, even though I try.

The Wilderness

Yet in the wilderness, Moses found a burning bush where God appeared to him. Moses noticed something unusual. Something caught his eye.

He stopped what he was doing. To step closer. And look.

The Scriptures tells us *God was watching Moses as he paused to turn.* Moses was curious. When God saw Moses drawing close, he spoke. God said the one word he had wanted to say from the moment he had placed the flame along the path.

"Moses."

God said his name.[1]

Your name. It's tattooed on the palm of his hand.

Your name. He writes it in his journal, the one he calls the Book of Remembrance.

Your name. He thought of you thousands of years ago as he lit a star in the sky, so it could twinkle back to you this night.

You can look out your window where the pale moonlight sails and hear him gently whispering to you—

I see you. I am here. In you.

Whitespace in Nature

Without uttering a single word, we can walk out into open spaces and hear Jesus whispering our names. By noticing the wild things around us, we can enjoy *spiritual whitespace in nature.*

It wasn't always like this for me. I've always enjoyed the outdoors, but it was limited to hiking trips with friends. I never intentionally sought soul conversations with God out in nature until he sent me to a desert one year.

I had to make trips out to Sedona, Arizona's Red Rock country, to help my mother get treatment for muscle pain. I was in my twenties, but I felt so old inside. The walls that followed me as a child still imprisoned me as an adult. I was miserable.

One night in Sedona, I couldn't fall asleep. I slipped out of bed, wrapped myself in layers, put on my boots, and quietly cracked the front door open. I went out to hike in the dead of night.

I stepped out and the moon stunned me. It was so big and bright. I had never stood in the desert lit up by a full moon. I could even see the arms of manzanita, luminescent and statuesque, sculpting my path.

The silence was so crisp, it spoke like a lover's voice on a lonely night. I climbed over rocks with ease and sat perched over a canyon. The jagged mountains climbed like a stairway from the creek up to the sky. Stars scattered like cookie crumbs in Oreo ice cream, twinkling like an endless Lite-Brite.

Everything stood so still. My soul took a breath and I could hear the gentle push of water running down somewhere below.

I began to cry. I'd never seen anything so wild and beautiful. What was staggering was that *it was all hidden*. While everyone slept in cities busy far away, God was awake in his creation.

What about me, God? I whispered. *Can I be beautiful too . . . hidden?*

As I wept without consolation, a passage floated to my mind:

The God who made the world and everything in it, this Master of sky and land . . . doesn't need the human race to run errands for him, as if he couldn't take care of himself. . . . *He made the earth hospitable, with plenty of time and space for living so we could seek after God.* (Acts 17:26–27 Message)

It was God saying to me—

I can take care of you, Bonnie.
I made this world beautiful, so you can find me.

Look into the wild things.
I have a place in this world for you.

That night, I wished I could have died right then and there, on that rock.

Then I would've left this world happy and free. But that wasn't the night God wanted me home.

God's Love Note: Beauty

Now I look into the wild things he makes so beautifully—to remind myself I was made for beauty. Ever since that night in Sedona, I've been returning to the outdoors. I long to be still enough to hear God speak to me again.

I might go for a walk or drive out to the coast to sit watching the ocean. *I go, looking to find one thing that captures my attention.* I hold it close as God's love note left just for me. Just like he did for Moses in the burning bush.

Out in the whitespace of nature, we can stop. We can escape the manufactured world. We leave the world others have designed for us to be with the One who designed beauty for us. He is the one who names the stars and carries your name in his heart.

God is waiting to meet us in the spiritual whitespace in nature. Will it be the breeze swirling your hair in your eyes he sends to touch you, or the swallow darting across your path?

You and I aren't nothing. We belong in the whitespace of God's creation.

God's Touch: Mystery

It takes faith to stop for beauty. To rest long enough to be curious. Then, maybe, we'll remember what it's like to notice something small. To feel God's touch and see what he sees.

185

As I sat there on red rock that night long ago, drinking in white-space, the night sky began to pale. I was watching my first dawn in the desert welcome me. I felt something I hadn't felt in a very, very long time.

Mystery.

I wondered if I could ever be that intimate and beautiful to God. Bare. In that moment, I longed for a different kind of rest other than death.

I longed for beauty.

And as I did the hard work of remembering my past, my soul was coming alive again. I had to make a decision. Should I go find my father?

> The heavens are telling of the glory of God;
> And their expanse is declaring the work of His hands.
> Day to day pours forth speech,
> And night to night reveals knowledge.
> There is no speech, nor are there words;
> Their voice is not heard. . . .
> In them He has placed a tent for the sun,
> Which is as a bridegroom coming out of his chamber. (Ps. 19:1–5)

Pull Up a Chair—Share

Are you longing for more beauty and mystery in your life?

How does being out in nature bring rest to your soul?

Share a memory of connecting with God in nature that touched your heart.

A Whitespace Prompt—Try This

Photo journal God's love notes. Meet with God in the spiritual whitespace of nature. What captures your attention? Tuck a camera in your pocket and take a walk out among the wild things. Make a photo journal of what moves you.

Don't worry about their significance or meaning. Just capture moments you've discovered. Don't worry about how much time you have. Let go of the pressure to make this a regular, repeatable "discipline." Just be prompted. Allow yourself to make space for mystery and beauty.

A Soul Conversation—Confide in Him

How did you cope with hard times as a little girl? What are the ways you try to disappear? Let Jesus know.

PART 5

whitespace
signifies
relationship

Rest Is a Living Journey

In architecture, space sculpts
the soul of a building,
creating places to rest and connect.
Whitespace is the breath of
relationship: *living spaces*.

19

torn

The Living Way

Oh, love that will not let me go. I rest my weary
soul in Thee. I trace the rainbow through the
rain.

George Matheson

I don't want to find my father.

That's what I told Dr. P. My dad left when I was seven. End of
story. Never came back to visit. I grew up just fine without him.

"Think back to the last time you saw your father," Dr. P asks.
"How did you feel then?" Of course I felt wrecked. Of course I
didn't want him to leave.

"You've been split from the moment your mother cut up those
photos of your father," Dr. P reflects. "But you can see from all
your memories, you loved your father."

I stand up to gather my things. It is the end of a session. "You're
a therapist. Of course you want me to reunite with my father. I don't
want to. Can you understand that? Maybe one day. Just not now."

I remind Dr. P I just want enough healing to write again, not to solve the cosmic question of a lost fatherhood. *Puh-leeze.* "It seems childish. Going back to find my father who never even bothered to look for me. He should be the one looking for me. Not the other way around." I grew more adamant by the second.

Finding my father was not part of my plan, until Dr. P leaves me with one question.

"Do you know if he's even still alive?"

As I pulled my car out of the parking lot, it struck me. I may never know what really happened. Maybe he was dead.

A Deeper Story

Torn. It's an uneasy place that keeps your heart in a perpetual loop. Imprisoned from entering into new chapters in your story. *A deeper story.*

Do you ever find yourself torn at times as well—between the story you've lived and a new story God's writing in you?

This deeper story lies in you and me. Without whitespace, there cannot be a new story.

> Jesus opened *a new and life-giving way* through the curtain into the Most Holy Place. (Heb. 10:20 NLT)

This living way.
It goes deep. To the most Holy Place. Sacred. Virgin.
Where no one can go. Except us, with Jesus. And Jesus in us.

A Living Journey: Relationship

In architecture, space sculpts the soul of a building, creating places for people to relax and relate. Whitespace makes room for connection, God's living story taking shape in you.

Whitespace is the breath of relationship: *living spaces.*

192

The journey of rest that Jesus opens for us is always new. Because it is organic, it wants to run deep, even though we may resist entering the whitespaces of our story.

We try to control the journey of what a restful life ought to look like. *But the journey of rest paved by faith is a living story.* It cannot be contained. It is beautifully mysterious and personal.

It's soul exhausting. To hold ourselves back from it. Because following this deeper journey into spiritual whitespace requires us to surrender to Someone. To one Person's voice, movement, and embrace.

Rest is not a lifestyle. Rest is a living journey: a relationship. *Resting is a relationship we walk by faith with Jesus into our most vulnerable places.*

Maybe, like me, you've made a life next to cut-up photographs. You've learned to fill in the blanks without giving your heart a chance to journey new. You separate that part of yourself from him and say, *I'm okay.* But Jesus whispers in return, *I am the way, the truth, and the life.*

We were made for the soul adventure of whitespace. "Call to me and I will answer you, and will tell you great and hidden things that you have not known" (Jer. 33:3 ESV).

Sometimes we can't rest until we look at why our heart feels torn. We have to choose a living story. Jesus is our companion for this journey. He understands what it's like to feel torn. He can travel torn with us today.

You and I were destined to journey off script. To walk with Jesus by faith into the whitespaces of our story—*to trace the rainbow through the rain.*

A Living Story

That night, after the kids got tucked in bed, I cleaned up the dishes and sat at the kitchen counter. Eric was out with his guys' small group that evening, so I settled into the stillness of the room. I knew Eric would support whatever path I chose, but I needed to decide.

I opened my laptop to stream some John Coltrane. It was a blue night. I fired up my browser and started typing.

I was Googling my father's name.

Even just spelling his name felt forbidden.

I rarely think of him. But ironically, during the most important times in my life, I had to. Every time I filled out college applications and later, when I applied for a visa as a missionary, I was reminded of this missing person. I didn't lay eyes on my birth certificate for many years until I stood in line at city hall with Eric to register a marriage certificate.

The State of California needed proof of my legal existence. To authenticate I was born to real people, I had to show I had a mother and a father. A woman and a man who had names and birthdates. That night, as I tapped away on my keyboard, I couldn't believe it was happening. In less than a heartbeat, search results flickered onto my computer screen.

Eight names appeared on a list. Located all across the United States.

Only one lived in my state, in my county.

His name appeared next to an address. Even a phone number.

My father was listed in the white pages. Sixty-nine years of age.

I decided to leave those cut-up photographs and choose a living story instead. To do it. To open the door of my heart where there is only whitespace staring back at me.

I may be completely destroyed by what I discover. But it was time. To see what was behind the door I've never wanted to open before.

I would call my father on the weekend. As I turned out the lights, lying sleepless on my bed that night, I felt Jesus fold my hand into his.

I have placed my rainbow in the clouds. It is the sign of my permanent promise to you. (Gen. 9:13 NLT 1996)

Pull Up a Chair—Share

What are times in your life where you've felt torn?

How is God leading you to a crossroads—in your today now—split in different directions?

A Whitespace Prompt—Try This

Live-action camera. Rather than making a list of the pros and cons for each choice, imagine a live-action camera traveling with you down each different story line. Journey through each path with Jesus, allowing him to join in your conflicting thoughts and potential outcomes.

What do you see happening? How does it make you feel? Confide in Jesus and imagine him there. How does he respond while watching it all happen with you? Let it happen. Let Jesus be present with you.

A Soul Conversation—Confide in Him

Which step takes you off script but dares you to experience a deeper, *living story?*

20

daddy

Rest in Your Story

So my prayer is that your story will have involved
some leaving and some coming home, some summer and some winter.

Donald Miller

I didn't do it for him.

I didn't even do it for me. I don't need a father anymore. I'm
all grown up.

I did it for her. The little girl in me. I needed to get answers
for her, so I dialed his number, the father whom I hadn't seen in
thirty-five years.

The phone rang. I was sitting in the bathroom when I made the
call, toilet seat down.

I didn't want my kids to hear. I told my oldest son, Josh, I never
knew my father. He left when I was really little and never came back.

Josh asked why. "I don't really know, sweetie." That's all I could say.

"Why don't you ask Grandma?" Josh asked between mouth chews of Oreo at the snack table.

"She won't tell me either. She'd get mad if I asked her," I answered nonchalantly, unloading the dishwasher. "It's been a mystery. You know?" I tell him kids don't always get the answers they want.

"Yeah," Josh nodded a little too emphatically. Then he tore off to play Legos, leaving a wake of cookie crumbs for me to clean up.

For now, seven-year-old Josh is satisfied with this answer. I don't tell him my mother forbade me to look for my father. I don't tell him what my mother said she'd do if she ever found out I tried to make contact with my father.

She'd pack everything up one day and drive off without telling me where, and take my sister with her. I'd come home from school to an empty house.

Because I was the only English-literate person in the house, I read all our mail. I knew, from a young age, we were living on a month-to-month lease. Momma could make good on her threat. I never dared to test her resolve.

I Never Dared

So my teeth clattered and my fingertips grew cold as I sat next to the shower door, holding my cell phone.

Shoot. Maybe it's too echo-ey in here. The phone rings. Before I changed my mind, a man picks up on the other end.

"Ha-low?" He sounds like he's answering outside somewhere.

"Hi. Is this so-and-so?" I start out. "This is Bonnie. Bonnie so-and-so." I use my maiden name. I'm hoping for a big reaction.

"What? Who ah you?" He sounds annoyed.

"This is Bonnie. Your daughter." I say it in English, because it feels grown up. I say it like I'm sitting in on a conference call at work, when I introduce myself to a room of strangers.

Silence.

"Hello?" I say again.

"Yeah?" He bellows. "What you want?" This wasn't going well. For a split moment, I want to hang up. I decide to speak Chinese, in case he mixed me up with another Bonnie.

"I don't want anything. I want to come meet you. That's all."

More silence. *Oh gosh. Maybe he thinks I'm still poor. Maybe he thinks I want his money or something.*

"I'm married now. With two boys. I just want to visit. Do you want to see me?" I'm biting my lip, trying not to cry.

"When you want to meet?" he asks.

Like strangers politely exchanging information off their car insurance papers at the scene of an accident, we agree on a time and place.

His home. The next day. Two o'clock in the afternoon.

In less than forty-eight hours, I went from being completely apathetic about the father who left me to inviting myself over to visit him the following day.

The Mission

That night, as Eric and I sat on our bed to come up with a game plan for the visit, it felt like we were the last two soldiers left in the trenches behind enemy lines. This was do or die.

"Look," Eric analyzes. He's an ex-Army military intelligence guy who turned techie. "It's impossible to know what he's thinking. You've got to figure out what *you* want to get out of this. What is the mission here?"

I didn't know, really. But one thing was for sure. I wasn't going to let him hurt me again.

I decided this would be a veiled reconnaissance to gather intel. A fact-finding mission. I would not go as a little girl. I would go as Lisa Ling, an investigative journalist.

I prepared a script. Why I'm here. What I'm requesting. I jotted a list of questions. *I can do this.*

The next morning, I texted a few friends to pray for me. They texted back shocked but encouraging words. This was a covert operation, but I needed friends to handle the carnage if I returned without limbs.

I needed backup, to get me out if things got bad. "I'm going with you," Eric said, holding me close. Quietly together, we cast our prayers into the dark the night before.

This Stranger

Spring was light that afternoon as we snaked our way into a neighborhood I'd never been. He lived so close, just two towns from mine. Fifteen minutes from where I grew up.

Here he was all along, and I never knew it. We saw the sun break in the morning and watched it set the same time at night. The reality of how near he lived pressed my heart up against my chest. I felt nervous and mixed up.

It was a nice neighborhood. Lawns trimmed. Houses that stood straight and tucked in. The cars parked along the street weren't beat up or up on cement blocks. There was no litter to confetti the gutters, so different from the streets I walked through as a little girl.

I was counting house numbers posted out in front. As we slowly pulled up along one curb, in front of an egg yolk–yellow house with white trim and clean windows, I saw him.

He was standing in the driveway, watching our car slow to a stop.

The way his body rested on his hips. His stance. The way his arms hung. His hair black and white sandy, stuck out choppy, falling on his face just so.

I recognize him, I say to myself.

It's him. My lips begin to tremble.

This stranger.

I know this man.

He's my daddy.

And I no longer feel sure about this meeting. I swing the car door open and I am shaking. My legs feel short and wobbly, my feet small.

It takes forever to touch the ground as I step out onto the curb. I feel dizzy. I feel like I'm going to trip and crumple under the weight of my body.

Don't Know Why

I remember the gifts I brought and walk to the back of the SUV like a robot. It's all so surreal. I'm dazed, because all I hear crying through me, over and again—like the crash of a gong vibrating through my skull—is this:

WHY did you . . . leave me?

Why . . . did you leave ME?

Why?

I try to gather bags of tangerines with one hand and a pink bakery box of pastries in the other. But I'm stumbling back there. I don't know why, but I feel angry. Sad and pitiful.

Like clones of Fred Flintstone the alien spacecraft discharges down onto earth to invade the planet, I stare blankly, programmed only to mechanically speak one phrase. Except it's not "yabba-dabba-doo" echoing in me.

Why did you leave? I wanted to wail it into the sky, run back in the car, and have Eric drive me far away. But I don't. I'm frozen.

I Remember

I picked tangerines to bring with me, because for the Chinese these shiny clusters of orange symbolize happiness and prosperity. A welcome sign to him of some sort. I chose Chinese pastries because I have a memory of him biting into one and because I love them too.

I carry these gifts to start our visit, to say, "Hello. How are you?" But as I walk closer, I look into his eyes for the first time. He dips his head to one side and stretches both arms out.

Before I could object, he folds me into his enveloping embrace. And I remember it all—the way his arms squeezed and how he patted my back.

Like a winter squall gusting across a swelling ocean, waves of decades-old memories pummel fresh through my body. I'm sucked back into a swirling blur of concrete driveway, shaking like a stick.

The Bonnie who went looking for answers fell to the wayside. *She disintegrated into the little girl I had long left behind, the one my father abandoned long ago.* I stood there as her now, holding on to Daddy, crying so hard my temples caved in and my heart shattered into a thousand pieces. Just like the day he left me.

I don't want him to hug me. But I can't say a thing. I can't swallow my weeping or quell the flashbacks flooding my heart.

I am angry he left. But I'm more embarrassed I'm falling apart in the very arms that let me go.

Devastated

My father says to us, "Come in. Come in," and points us to enter the house through the garage door. A Chinese woman with her hair pulled back steps out to greet us. He introduces her as his wife. She acts chipper and friendly, like a hostess at a restaurant showing you to your table. I notice how clean and well-kept each room is. Not at all like the bum my mother always said my father was. I'm confused by everything.

My father has hardly said a word to me or shed a tear. So, the first thing I ask him, before we sit down in the living room, is this,

"Do you recognize me? Do you . . . remember me?" My voice is fragile, because my nose is stuffy and my eyes are puffy.

He glances at me sideways. Takes a long hard look. He begins to slowly . . . shake his head. No, he says without speaking.

And I start breaking into an ugly cry. I cover my face in my hands and collapse into a white leather sofa.

He doesn't recognize me.

He doesn't even know me.

This time, I'm totally, completely devastated.

I thought about bolting through the front door. But I couldn't just stand up and do that. Could I? I wished Eric would get up and tell my father, "I'm sorry. We'd better go now." But we were speaking in Chinese and he had no idea what was being said.

I felt so alone, sitting there doubled over, bawling next to an old man who really was a stranger and my sweet husband who couldn't help me.

The Daddy I remember isn't here anymore. That Daddy is gone.

I have no daddy. I silently howled as bitter tears poured.

I'm all alone. Just like it's always been.

The little girl in me is abandoned. Again.

The Weight of Stress

I don't know if you've ever felt devastated like me, if it's led you to do as I've done. To write a script. To take on roles that fit the occasion. To find a mission you can follow. So you don't have to ask the whys.

You'd understand the tremendous burden of keeping your suffering locked away, because it doesn't seem spiritual to brush near the truth of your devastation. You'd carry the weight of stress to keep your story at bay.

We are afraid to face the truth about ourselves. Our past, dreams, break-ups, fathers and mothers, addictions, and stories of brokenness. The shame. Of what we've done. Of what was done to us.

We want to obliterate it. We don't want our worst fears to come true. No one would want us. No one would love us anymore.

So we become fragments of stories. We are not whole.

Rest in Your Story

I'm learning the broken stories in us don't go away. I asked Jesus why he would want me to find my father and wound me a second time.

Jesus wanted me to, so my story doesn't have to hide in shame.

Come to Me, all who are weary and heavy-laden, and I will give you rest. (Matt. 11:28)

My story can rest out in the open with him. Jesus doesn't tell us to fix it. Get over it. He accepts our pain. He honors our brokenness. He says—

I want that. What nobody else wants. What nobody values.
Your story.
I love the real you.
I have called you by name. You are mine (Isa. 43:1).
I will carry you (46:4).

The Mission of Whitespace

Let your heart rest from holding back your story. No more running away. Let God write in the whitespaces, as you face the unknown with him.

Jesus will carry you through the whitespaces because *God's mission in spiritual whitespace is you. Your heart is God's mission field. He wants to reach you where you're unreached.*

This mission is unpredictable. That's why we need each other for the journey.

Jesus Knows

As your *whys* dangle unanswered, imagine Jesus confiding in us too—

I've tasted rejection and choked out my whys.
  I cried out on the cross in anguish—
  Daddy . . . don't you love me? Why have you forsaken me?
  I heard no reply.
  The Father turned away that moment, when everything
broken cut through me.
  No one to hold me. Not even a father.

Jesus knows that not every *why* has a happy ending. For every broken part of your story, he was living it for an eternity, hanging on the cross. And he lives it again in you now, as he walks you through it today.

Some say a person's life flashes before them during the last seconds before they die. I wonder what flashed before Jesus's eyes? Could it have been scenes from our stories that devastate us—could *those* be the stories that flashed before him on the cross?

Surely our griefs He Himself bore,
And our sorrows He carried. (53:4)

His wounds didn't disappear with his resurrected body. *Jesus chose to walk out into the world with his scars from the past—visible.*

It's with those hands he reaches out to gently hold you and draw you to his side, where his other scar is tender, where water and blood flowed. So you can touch it and know that you are safe.

Show him where the life drains out of you. Where you are empty beyond empty.

As you do, press into him. Gaze into his eyes as he whispers—

Don't be afraid. I've traveled this journey of pain too.
I understand you. I know how you feel.

For we do not have a high priest who is unable to empathize with our weaknesses, but we have one who has been tempted in every way, just as we are—yet he did not sin. (Heb. 4:15 NIV)

Pull Up a Chair—Share

What are the scripts you've written for yourself to play?

How are you carrying the weight of anxiety?

A Whitespace Prompt—Try This

Echo your whys. Honor them. Write out the story where your *whys* ring loudest in your soul from the past or today.

A Soul Conversation—Confide in Him

Unburden your heart from all the fear and shame you may be carrying about the *whys* that have not led to a storybook ending. Jesus understands your journey of pain.

21

lost and found

Awakening

The face of all the world is changed, I think,
Since first I heard the footsteps of thy soul
Move still, oh, still, beside me.

Elizabeth Barrett Browning

I cried for an eternity on the sofa.

Then he spoke. "I'm sorry Daddy wasn't there. Daddy didn't take care of you." I reached for the box of Kleenex on the coffee table, to wipe my eyes and blow my nose.

"I tried to visit, but all that fighting. You and your sister screaming and crying. What could I do?" He sat back and folded his hands in his lap.

I felt sorry for him. But then I remembered my script. My investigative reporting.

"Can you tell me what happened, between you and Momma?" I parked my sad little self to the side, to get some answers.

He was quiet for a while. "Your momma said I was good for nothing. I'm uneducated, poor with no future. Useless." He talked as if he was far away, but I knew the voice he was speaking of, the same sharp blade against my soul.

"Uh-huh." I nodded.

"She said if I had anything left of a man in me, I'd give her a divorce." Total shock. Richter scale reading: 8.0. My mother had told me he divorced her, that *he* left us.

He continued. "She said I was ugly. That she couldn't stand the sight of me. She hated me. All that yelling. I couldn't take it anymore. That's no life. I can't be happy. So, I said, 'Okay. Divorce.'"

So he left because he wasn't happy. My heart beat crazy, like a jackhammer pounding against asphalt.

The Hidden City

"Did you ever wonder about me?" My eyes began to well up. This question was not on my list. "You never came back to see me. Why didn't you ever write?"

My father shrugged. "That's what your momma said she wanted. So, I figured. Fine. You want a divorce. That's what you'll get."

I broke down into a puddle of nothing. I didn't want post-traumatic stress from this meeting, so I let out the words.

"All these years. You didn't even send me a birthday card. If Momma kept you away, why didn't you come find me when I grew up?" The dam had broken. "I actually looked for you on graduation day in high school. I thought maybe you'd come. I thought maybe. . . ."

I couldn't finish my sentence. *That hidden city I'd been erecting all these years—the walls I erected to protect myself—it was all crumbling.* On every side.

207

I was a sputtering mess. "I thought you might have had cancer. Maybe you were dead. . . . We were so poor, we didn't even have money to see the doctors." My nose was so stuffy, I couldn't enunciate.

"And you've been here all along," I eeked, choking into sobs as she tumbled out of me messy, pathetic, and shameless. The little girl in me.

"That's what your momma wanted." This was becoming my father's refrain.

There was no point going any further. I began to collect myself now.

It's Over

The best way to describe this moment is a really bad break-up. You know, that sick feeling that hits you when you're bawling your eyes out because someone is breaking up with you? And you think, maybe if they knew how much they're ruining your life, they'd take you back? How you can't eat or sleep. How you can't do anything but cry.

But then you look over at the person who just trampled your soul. You look in their eyes and you feel it. You know it. The person who once loved you, whom you still love, doesn't love you anymore.

And you get it. *It's over.* That person who once loved you is no longer sitting in front of you. He's gone. He's not ever going to kiss you again.

That's when you do your best to clean yourself up, smooth out your hair, and take a big, shaky breath. So you can say goodbye. You make parting small talk, to show you're not going to grovel anymore.

That's what I did. I blew my nose to clear it one last time and I tell him, "You know, I do have some wonderful memories of you, Daddy. They make me happy when I think of them."

I tell him about the time I rubbed his toothbrush on a bar of soap until it got foamy and told him his toothbrush was ready. My daddy let out a holler I'll never forget over the bathroom sink. He rushed out and hugged me close, "Did you try to make Daddy eat soap?!" I remember how I threw my head back and roared with crazy laughter.

I tell him I remember the beautiful pink outfit. The wonton noodle soup we'd slurp in the noodle shop in Chinatown. And the toy he bought for me.

My father tries to smile. Too politely. *He doesn't remember.*

Goodbye

"You have a very nice house. . . . How is your health? Are you doing well?" I'm preparing my closing comments. The interview is over. And now, it's important to be a good houseguest. I turn to Eric, to translate. Eric gets my signal. He nods back and puts his hand on my shoulder.

"Yes, I bought it in 1984," my father says in English. He smiles now, for the first time. "My wife and I bought this place together. We've worked hard to pay it off. I'm retired now. Just three years ago."

I smile back. *1984.* I was fourteen then, struggling below the poverty line, living in my private misery.

"And this. This is my son." He hands me a picture of a Chinese guy garbed in a black cap and gown. His college graduation. My father stands on one side, his wife on the other. No one took my picture when I graduated from college. My mother said it was a waste of time, sitting there in the stands for hours in the heat. *Just for a piece of paper you could pick up at the offices.*

"That's wonderful," I reply.

My father starts telling me about his son, how he's working in high tech, married, with a house across town. He doesn't ask

209

about me, about how I'm doing, what I'm doing now, or whether I even went to college.

I thank him for his time and his hospitality. But we need to pick up our kids now. It's time for dinner. We'd better go.

As we stand at the doorway to leave, my father says to me, "Be happy. Forget about the old stuff." *Yes, yes, yes.* I nod.

As I close the car door and Eric starts the ignition, I sit there empty-handed. My father did not have any gifts prepared for me.

As we make a U-turn to exit the neighborhood, all I can think of is this—*My daddy didn't love me. My momma didn't either.*

I started crying. Because this time I really was saying goodbye in the driveway.

Lost

Maybe you can relate in some way to not feeling like you were loved. Like you were nobody's child. Sometimes, there comes a season in life where we can't deny it any longer.

We can't undo our story. We face the truth that we are lost in the world and irrevocably broken.

Jesus has words for people like us, orphaned by sadness in life.

Jesus tells a story—to those who were living good and shiny lives, who didn't understand why he spent so much time with people living broken stories, naming them as friends.

Jesus told me this story as I careened toward the trunk of an old oak tree the next morning, to sob into the bark because I couldn't take another step.

I wish I never saw him. I wish I never knew. . . . I stood there crying out to Jesus.

And like a gentle breeze blowing through the window as you lie sleepless in the heat of a long summer eve, I remember someone else walking a sun-scorched hill.

His sandals are dry and dusty. He has been looking for a very long time. He is anxious. He is desperately searching for the face of one who was missing when he counted ninety-nine.

He remembers the freckle on the pink near her nose. He knows she must be tired. Thirsty. Fallen in a ravine. Hungry and scared. Alone.

He says she is worth leaving the ninety-nine for. Because she isn't an investment to him; he isn't looking for an ROI. He loves her. She is his.

She is worth leaving everything for. He leaves happiness, comfort, and safety. *He risks it all.*

You know who he is.

This is the story of the Good Shepherd. He is Jesus. And he's left it all to find us.

Found

You. Me. Jesus pours oil on our wounds. Brings water to our parched lips.

Jesus puts us on his shoulders and carries us back home. Because he knows our names; he calls us "mine."

This isn't just a story told thousands of years ago. Jesus tells this story of being lost and found in mysteriously beautiful ways again *today*, in a gazillion different ways. He does this by unleashing this story to the world through your life. And mine.

Not just once when we first believed. This story is being written new and fresh every time we face into the truth of our lives, no matter how hard or broken it looks to others, even to ourselves.

Lost, then found. This is the Good News that *goes deeper* every time we dare to live out who God made us to be in this world. Walking by faith. Placing our trust in him.

Jesus calls us to follow him. To go where he leads us. And we

211

do, because his voice is different from the voices that have hurt and deserted us.

We can move out of the gate because he goes before us. He'll carry us back when we fall. You and I were meant to go on new journeys, to pursue desires God plants in our hearts. Let's unearth the dreams we've long lost, buried.

Life is organic. It's not always plastic, shiny, and perfect. Life changes like the seasons. This living way, after all, is a Person.

Rest comes from awakening our hearts to fully open up in our relationship with Jesus. Like all great loves, this relationship is filled with great risk and promise. To be named, to be claimed, by a Father who meets us in the driveway, after we've been discarded.

He is our real Father. He opens his arms. He says—*I choose you. I love you.*

And he's not letting go.

Nobody's Child

Nobody's child. These are the words echoing in my heart, as I lowered my body into a steaming bath that evening. As I slipped my feet under the covers and laid my head down, I began to weep.

Jesus . . . Jesus . . .
All my life, I've been waiting for someone to love me.
Now I know why.
It's true.
No one loved me.
But you chose me. When I was four in the basement, seven in the driveway, and seventeen in the hallway. And you choose me now at forty-two, sunken in trauma and anxiety.
You chose me in all those moments. And you choose me now.

I cried and I cried. Because this time, hope flickered to life. Because a peace that's never been mine touched me. Because this time, I recognized my tears as the sound of my heart breaking open and free.

There, in the deepest whitespace in my soul, I felt him whisper—

You are my child.
Beloved by God.

I was no longer nobody's child. It was always him. God chose me.

Your Heart's Homecoming

Sometimes you have to suffer the pain of the past to realize who you truly belong to. Whitespace is allowing ourselves to face *what* we've lost in order to believe that *we* can be found again.

Making room for whitespace is listening to that whisper-thin Voice that calls to you: *You have a new home with me now. Rest in the journey of your heart's homecoming.*

It is not easy to journey this new way, because it feels safer to stay where we've been. I think back to that little girl out on the driveway. I walk over to her, kneel, and tell her gently, "Jesus is here. Let him take you in his arms now. You have a new home. Come. Let's go."

This is the conversation I have so I can take small steps to nurture my spirit, care for my body, eat something warm and good, bring myself to be with others, drive myself to the beach, buy lavender chamomile tea, turn on some music, and journal at night. This is my new adventure: recapturing what's been lost, to return to being with the One I belong to: loved by Jesus, resting and free.

Awakening

This journey of rest doesn't happen overnight. I have to begin this soul adventure each and every day. Many times in the course of a day. Especially at night.

I'm trusting over time that this new rest—this new journey of my heart's homecoming—will feel more familiar. I know my struggle and restlessness won't go away completely until I'm finally home. Then I will see my Father face-to-face, each and every second of my every waking hour.

> So there is a special rest still waiting for the people of God. For all who enter into God's rest will find rest from their labors, just as God rested after creating the world. Let us do our best to enter that place of rest. (Heb. 4:9–11 NLT 1996)

Take this journey of your heart's awakening. Look into the eyes of your real Father. Trust him one moment at a time, enough to take one step into your life as the little girl who is beloved. Even if that movement is oh so small.

Because you and I are women whose hearts are full of dreams and desires that are still alive and young. And for the times we feel old and frail, we can rest in the One who calls us *his*.

> Suppose one of you has a hundred sheep and loses one of them. Doesn't he leave the ninety-nine in the open country and go after the lost sheep until he finds it? And when he finds it, he joyfully puts it on his shoulders and goes home. (Luke 15:4–6 NIV)

> Even to your old age and gray hairs
> I am he, I am he who will sustain you.
> I have made you and I will carry you. (Isa. 46:4 NIV)

Pull Up a Chair—Share

How are you in the middle of a "lost, then found" story?

Are you on a journey of saying goodbye somehow?

Are you on a journey of your heart's homecoming?

Share how God is prompting you to rest more fully with him.

A Whitespace Prompt—Try This

Awaken your heart. Sometimes the hidden cities we build, the walls we erect to protect ourselves, need to crumble in order to discover that God can carry us—to free us for a new journey.

How is God awakening your heart again in

love?

friendship?

marriage?

dating?

family?

your career?

church?

your health?

a dream?

A Soul Conversation—Confide in Him

What do you need for this journey for your heart to find a new home? Tell Jesus. He wants you to know he hears.

22

your whitespace story

Heart Set Free

I have been seized by the power of a great affection.

Brennan Manning

When Josh asks what I'm writing, I tell him he can read it later when he's older.

I tell Josh this is a book with some hard, grown-up stories. Stories that are kind of sad. Not for little kids. I tell my seven-year-old son I'm writing these stories because I want others to know how I'm finding Jesus through tough times and how Jesus is finding me.

I tell him I'm writing to encourage, to let others know Jesus is with them too, that it's okay to be sad when times are tough. God will always be with them. No matter what.

"I still want to read it," Josh says, munching on a chocolate chip granola bar in the backseat on the ride home after school.

"You will, sweetie. You will," I assure him.

The Only Way

After I saw my father, I was free of panic attacks for the first time in a year. I was finally sleeping without being violently jolted awake. For two weeks, I was euphoric.

So I thought I'd get back to writing my book, because the deadline for my manuscript was staring me in the face again. It had been the third time the publisher graciously extended the deadline. But as I attempted to write, it triggered more panic attacks.

I didn't understand. *What is it with this book?*

"Think back to when you last experienced panic attacks while writing. How did you feel?" Dr. P asks.

"Jumbled. Scared. I don't know why." I start feeling the anxious feelings.

Before Dr. P comments, it hits me.

"It's the little girl in me. I'm trying to write without her." I was trying to write separated from my wounded self. I didn't want to tell her story. Once it's out, it can never be gone. I didn't want her story to become a part of mine.

So I made the awful decision. *I can't write the old book.* It was the book the old me dreamed up, and I couldn't go back the way I had come.

I told my publisher the only chance I had to write my book now was to write it broken, with the little girl in me. This wasn't about writing a book any longer. There were other things I had to die to, if I wanted to really be free.

New Territory

I haven't had any full-blown panic attacks at night since I decided to put aside the old book. It doesn't mean I sleep soundly every night. I still have to take Ambien. It also doesn't mean I don't have anxiety attacks. I can drive, grocery shop, put on my earrings and

217

some blush, laugh, and carry on a conversation. I don't choke and I'm not leveled to the floor.

But when triggered, my heart pounds erratically, my chest tightens, and breathing is hard. I feel numb. Fatigued. I get nauseated and my tummy hurts. My neck tightens and I get a headache. I don't want to go anywhere or see anyone. I just want to stay at home.

It doesn't happen every day. But it still happens.

Dr. P tells me it's okay. "More of you is breaking through. You're continuing to heal."

This is all new territory. I'm unsure about who I am now, with all these recovered memories. I have to learn to walk into this world again, new, with the little girl in me.

I understand why my panic attacks have stopped. I describe it as traveling in a time machine. Parts of me, frozen in trauma, have been stuck. So I had to go back into the past to find her. PTSD has been my means of transport there.

By reliving my memories, I found the little girl holding all the broken pieces, alone. Abandoned and unloved. *The moment I made the choice to find my father in my "now" time, I took that little girl out of the past and brought her into the present.* She's finally safe because her wounds don't have to be hidden anymore. She is real.

I am seeing her for who she really is. A girl nobody really saw, but God did. There was no convenient, un-messy way for me to find her. But now that I have, I am free to rest.

The little girl is here now and God is using her to change my plans.

What's at Stake

"Does that mean I have a split personality or something?" I ask Dr. P. "Am I going crazy?"

"No." Dr. P chuckles. I crack him up, apparently. "If you can ask whether you're crazy, you're not," Dr. P quips. Therapist humor.

Dr. P explains that multiple personality disorder is a mental illness where you lose touch with reality, with who you are. "You'd be talking in voices of different people and not even know it," he said.

"Okay. That's good." I sighed with relief.

"What is happening to you is a beautiful thing, Bonnie. God's bringing all the parts of you back to life. Abundant life."

That little girl in me is here now and I can't put her away. It's affecting everything I do. I have to make new choices, and make them for different reasons.

If I try to revert to my old ways of coping—saying yes when I should say no, powering through, ignoring my heart and my body, going somewhere out of guilt, living off to-do lists because it's more efficient—I get stressed. Really anxious.

I can't do the old way anymore. My heart won't let me. *I need whitespace.*

I'm sharing this important juncture in my story to let you know the journey of faith sets your heart free. It gets deeper. And the deeper it goes, the more what's at stake emerges.

You. Jesus in you.

We can't go back the way we came. *Let's travel ahead with each other—to awaken our hearts to rest in whitespace, to recover those pockets of our real selves.*

Each time we take time to rest, to crack the door to our hearts a bit, we will find her. The little girl inside us all.

At the Very Center of Life

"Will that little girl in me ever grow up?" I asked Dr. P.

"No. She'll always be with you. She won't always be so sad.

But she's you, Bonnie. That little girl is who God made you."
Dr. P smiles.

I'm kind of sad when I hear this. Now that the genie's out
of the bottle, I'm not sure what all this means. Because making
space to nurture and care for the little girl in me does not fit into
my picture of being a faith-filled follower of Jesus. I want to be
mature, unruffled by stress and anxiety. Filled with peace that
makes me strong, unaffected by worry. I don't want to be needy,
like a child.

It reminds me of the disciples. Was that how they felt as wild,
pint-sized children zip-zagged around their parents to approach
Jesus? Children are loud, unpredictably excitable. They get tired,
whiny, and hungry, and talk about random things at the most pe-
culiar moments.

The children were hoping Jesus would touch them. The disciples
were annoyed and impatient for them to go away.

> But Jesus was irate and let them know it: "Don't push these children
> away. Don't ever get between them and me. *These children are at
> the very center of life in the kingdom.* Mark this: Unless you ac-
> cept God's kingdom in the simplicity of a child, you'll never get
> in." Then, gathering the children up in his arms, he laid his hands
> of blessing on them. (Mark 10:13–16 Message)

Jesus was telling me, ever so clearly—

Awaken your heart.
   The little girl in you stands at the very center of my heart.
   Let me take her in my arms and bless her.
   Rest in whitespace with me.
   Each time you do, you bring me pleasure.

It's casting a whole new light on the importance of creating
whitespace. He wants me to spend time with him as his little girl,

rather than pushing her out of the way because I'm too busy or stressed. To feel God's pleasure is the ultimate blessing waiting for us when we make room for whitespace.

Hearts Free

And without faith it is impossible to please God, because anyone who comes to him must believe that he exists and that he rewards those who earnestly seek him. (Heb. 11:6 NIV)

The world calls us to hide our stressed-out selves. But Jesus calls us to a radical new rest: *Draw near. As is.*

Jesus invites us into a new relationship to set our hearts free.

Jesus wants us to bring him what's real and worrisome as well as what's simple and beautiful. *A child brings all parts of herself to Jesus.* She can't help it. That's the way she is.

Anyone who becomes as humble as this little child is the greatest in the Kingdom of Heaven. *And anyone who welcomes a little child like this on my behalf is welcoming me.* (Matt. 18:4–5 NLT)

This blows me away. *When we welcome the child in us, and in others, we are welcoming the very presence of Jesus.* This is what we get to do in spiritual whitespace.

It's mind-boggling. It makes my skin tingle and my heart quicken with amazement. Taking time for whitespace to rest, create, and play—to laugh, enjoy friends, see new places, and explore new adventures—is heart-freeing faith.

When you're struggling with your day, feeling down, stressed out, or frazzled, *help that little girl inside.*

Offer her the whitespace she longs for.

Bring her to Jesus.

Remind yourself of the beauty in whitespace, the beauty of God in your story.

Come join me.

The Next Chapter

Our time together isn't over yet. I want to invite you to awaken your soul to rest.

Let's take the journey to set our hearts free alongside each other. Because I don't want to do it alone.

Turn with me to part 6. Gather your stories—the ones you've uncovered between the pages of this book—and let's walk the little girls in us out into the world.

Take the Whitespace Challenge with me. How? Let me tell you what I mean.

> Strengthen me according to your word. . . .
> I hold fast to your statutes, O Lord;
>   do not let me be put to shame.
> *I run in the path of your commands,*
>   *for you have set my heart free.*
> (Ps. 119:28, 31–32 NIV 1984)

Pull Up a Chair—Share

How do you feel about the little girl in you?

Are you longing for God to free your heart?

A Whitespace Prompt—Try This

The little girl. Is there something you can do in your "now" time for the little girl in you? Free your heart—to discover who God's always made you to be.

A Soul Conversation—Confide in Him

Picture yourself bringing the little girl to Jesus right now. Speak to him as her. Because she is you. She stands at the center of God's kingdom and in Jesus's heart.

PART 6

the whitespace challenge

Rest Is an Awakening

Simplicity and repose are the qualities that
measure the true value of any work of art.
Frank Lloyd Wright

23

a new ambition

When you have laboriously accomplished your
daily task, go to sleep in peace. God is awake.

Victor Hugo

One challenge nobody warned me about when I became starry-
eyed pregnant was how laundry would soon become a stumbling
block. Literally. I walk by the hallway where our laundry baskets
are lined up and it looks like raccoons got into them. Two, to be
exact. One who is seven and the other, still in preschool, who acts
like he's seven.

Some days I just give up.

I'm never caught up anyway. The weekend comes and my pile
has exploded into a mountain of socks, jeans, and regret. I only
wish I could go outside and play. Instead, I end up folding clothes,
listening to the washer and dryer turn the house into a laundromat.

Stress feels the same. I wake up and stress greets me, just like
that pile of laundry. Sometimes I walk right by and refuse to acknowledge its existence. It can't touch me.

Eventually I'll find myself trapped and surrounded by one anxious thought after another.

A Different Kind of Stress

Can we ever be free from stress? Stress seems to be so embedded in our modern lives, we've come to breathe it like oxygen.

Emails, Twitter, doctor appointments, and a to-do list filled with growing unchecked boxes are all part of my reality.

Is it realistic to expect a stress-free life?

I've lived a lot of my life hiding from my heart, reducing everything to a minimum. I did *do* less. But paring down to the bare essentials made me lose a sense of wonder.

Introverts or extroverts, we were never made to only do life as maintenance. God designed us to be fully alive: *creative, renewed by a sense of adventure, engaged with community, and soul-fed.*

Without these elements of creativity, adventure, community, and soul care, we experience a different kind of stress.

Soul stress.

I don't want to make a reentry into striving a stream of new endeavors either, like stepping into the California rivers for whitewater rafting. Everything looks calm on the outside, but the underlying currents threaten to pull me under.

Are we left to choose only between inactivity or overactivity?

As people of faith, our focus goes beyond avoiding stress.

We pursue the opposite.

We pursue rest.

A New Ambition

After PTSD entered my life, I couldn't socialize with people like I used to or do life like I once did. I could hardly keep track of my car keys.

228

I look out from my post-PTSD life and all I see is desert. I see nothing.

What do I do with my life? What do I do with these empty spaces?

You'd think the concept of whitespace came through some inspiring moment walking through a field of wildflowers. But "feeding my soul" sounded too right-brain. Too touchy-feely. So God prompted my first steps through what was initially most accessible: my left brain.

God knew this about my personality: my desire to pursue. So he put me on the journey to rest *by pointing me to a new ambition*. It's ironic. The idea of spiritual whitespace came to me while reading a blog on business strategies and innovation.

I was reading an article written by Matthew May called "Break Through by Taking Breaks." It offered scientific evidence that downtime is required for creativity and new thinking. Archimedes discovered volume displacement while taking a bath. Einstein's theory of special relativity came while he was daydreaming, and author J. K. Rowling sat traveling on a train when the Harry Potter character "flashed in her mind."[1]

> Ever wonder why our best ideas come when we're in the shower, driving, daydreaming, or sleeping? . . . When you look deeper into these brilliant flashes of insight you can see they came at strange times and in random locations. They didn't occur while actually working on the problem but after an intense, prolonged struggle with it *followed by a break. A change of scene and time away played a part.*[2]

It was fascinating to learn that "putting pressure on ourselves to try and work harder, more intensely, or more quickly may only slow down our ability to arrive at new insights."[3]

If this is true in the worlds of art and science, what would be the implications for our relationships with God—in spirituality and faith? The biggest lightbulb moment struck me. I had been desperately trying to connect with God by doing the same things. I thought I needed to try harder.

What's wrong with me?

Nothing. I needed something different.

Rest as Ambition

I typed in *rest* into my computer to do a word search in the Bible. What I found stunned me to the core.

Rest. It sounds inactive, doesn't it? I was surprised to find that *rest is one of only three ambitions that God explicitly calls out in the Bible.* The other two are preaching the gospel and pleasing God.[4]

> We urge you, brethren, to excel still more, and to make it your ambition to lead a quiet [restful] life. (1 Thess. 4:10–11)

Turns out *hesuchazo*—the Greek word used for *quiet* and *rest*—is *as important* as preaching the gospel and pleasing God. The more I'm able to enjoy rest, the more others will see God's life in me. When my soul is at rest, I am free to please God right where I am.

I was intrigued. I had always centered my thinking on pleasing God and preaching the gospel *through what I did*. But now, suddenly God put a big spotlight on *hesuchazo*. God was asking me to excel—"still more"—by making it my ambition to lead a quiet and restful life.

My heart skipped a beat. This is what has been missing. Rest.

Hesuchazo became the match that ignited the fire of the Holy Spirit in spiritual whitespace.

We were never made to only do life as maintenance. God designed us to be fully alive: creative, engaged with community, and renewed by a sense of adventure.

As people of faith, our focus goes beyond avoiding stress. We pursue the opposite. We pursue rest.

Our ambition is spiritual rest.

Ten Prompts for Soul Rest

I was so intrigued by the ambition to rest, I looked up Scriptures using the word *rest* and categorized them into four buckets: *creativity, adventure, community,* and *soul care.*

I started brainstorming different ways to enjoy rest and created a "Spiritual Whitespace Menu." They became ten brews—ten prompts—to rejuvenate and feed my soul.

It was amazing. It was like discovering new roasts of coffee beans, a lifetime's worth to explore and savor. Spending time to rest with God caffeinates the life of faith.

Spiritual whitespace is a creative way of spending time with God to slow down and feed your soul, to rejuvenate and enjoy soul rest.

My heart felt so weary and lonely, but walking through it all, I found a new journey so invigorating that it's forever changed my heart and my story.

I took the *Whitespace Challenge*—and now, I'm inviting you to take this challenge with me today.

What is the rest you are most craving? Will you take the Whitespace Challenge?

Turn with me to the next chapter. Let's explore the Spiritual Whitespace Menu. Join me. Take the Whitespace Challenge to rejuvenate your soul. I've placed whitespace prompts to get you started and blank spaces to add your own ideas, based on journaling you've done in previous chapters.

Ready? I hope you'll feel your soul stirring. It's the movement of God's presence, longing to bring you rest.

Explore what your soul currently craves. Enjoy a shot of rest.

Pull Up a Chair—Share

How are you longing for *hesuchazo*—for quiet, for rest?

Which of the four elements of *spiritual whitespace* is your soul craving today: creativity, adventure, community, or soul care?

A Whitespace Prompt—Try This

Inject some ambition. How can you add an "ambitious" element to cultivate rest?

Left brain. How can you use your left brain more (be more analytical or objective) to be more restful?

Right brain. Alternatively, how can you use your right brain more (be more intuitive, emotional, or creative) to help you lead a quieter life?

A Soul Conversation—Confide in Him

Have you felt disconnected with God, even though you know how you ought to feel? How would you like things to be between you and him?

24

a menu

What

While reading Matthew May's article, I noticed a pen and ink stipple portrait—a type of drawing iconic to the *Wall Street Journal* called a *hedcut drawing*. You know, the drawing printed next to an article to show what the columnist looks like? A hedcut portrait illustrates a person's face mostly by the use of whitespace and "artfully placed dots and dashes—and the brain fills in the rest."[1]

It's the whitespace that gives you the picture. I've been trying so hard to fill in the blanks that I've lost my picture. What room have I left for God to make his dots on me?

If I gave him a little more space in my heart and in my schedule, would I begin to see his image emerge—one tiny dot at a time?

Whitespace Tasting

I was curious. I didn't know how long it would take for his portrait to be etched. No matter. The Artist knows. That's how I took my first shot of spiritual whitespace.

It's time now for you.

Don't worry about *how* you'll brew your cup of rest or whether you'll consume it regularly. Resist the urge to turn this into a test of your will.

Engage your heart.

Right now, just brainstorm *what* your whitespace looks like in your season of faith.

Imagine yourself standing at an espresso bar during a coffee tasting event where the barista is serving up samples of whitespace roasts, brewed hot and fresh. Just for you.

Keep in mind your personal whitespace story and *explore what your soul currently craves.*

Sip long and slow. Breathe in the aroma. Try different whitespaces.

The more you taste, the more the palate of your soul will come alive to the many subtle flavors of rest.

Spiritual Whitespace Menu:
Ten Prompts to Awaken Your Soul to Rest

Spiritual whitespace: a creative way of spending time with God to slow down and feed your soul, to rejuvenate and enjoy soul rest. The four elements of spiritual whitespace are creativity, adventure, community, and soul care.

Creativity

Enjoy a Creative Cappuccino. A delicious espresso of creative whitespace poured into the artistic you, etching artful patterns of rest onto your soul.

1. **Creative Exploration.** Take time out for God's art in you.

Engage in activity where you are free to be, without needing to be functional or to judge how you are doing.

For the one who has entered His rest has himself also rested from his works, as God did from His. (Heb. 4:10)

Ideas

☐ *What did you enjoy* doing naturally as a little girl?

☐ *Drive yourself to the store* and buy that little girl in you some supplies.

☐ *Pick up your camera*, brush, pen, spatula, whisk, or scissors, along with paper, basil, flour, yarn, or fabric and move your soul through your fingers.

☐ *Listen to live music* at a café, open-air concert, or jazz club.

☐ *Explore your creative interest* through browsing books, watching a documentary, or taking a one-time workshop.

☐ *Start that blog.* Just for you.

☐ _____

2. **A Creative Whitespace Getaway.** Stop from your daily routine to feed your soul. Enjoy a change of everyday scenery. Take the time to enjoy soulful places with Jesus.

Come away by yourselves to a secluded place and rest a while. (Mark 6:31)

Ideas

☐ *Roam* an antique store, a sandy beach, or the hallways of an art exhibit.

☐ *Drive* a little farther out to walk and journal under tree limbs on a Saturday.

☐ *Take a bite* of a morning croissant at a café.

☐ *Sit outside* on your patio with tea and honey under the stars late one night.

☐ _____

Adventure

Enjoy an Adventure Latte. A generous shot of God's rest steamed with his presence, sweetened with your pick of adventure for added flavor.

3. **Moving Things.** Enjoy God in your new endeavors. That's what Moses insisted. Time to leave and journey into a new chapter with God.

My presence shall go with you, and I will give you rest. (Exod. 33:14)

Ideas

☐ *What is a move* you've felt restless to explore but have been avoiding in your job, hobby, lifestyle, health/fitness, relationship, community, or ministry?

☐ *De-clutter your house.* Create a soulful home to reflect your "now" life.

☐ *De-clutter your heart.* What is the cargo (expectations, relationships, beliefs, goals, plans) you need to jettison or the lifeboat you must cut loose?

☐ _____

4. **The Wild Things.** Enjoy the outdoors, soaking up nature. Bring your body and senses to rest.

The whole earth is at rest and is quiet;
They break forth into shouts of joy. (Isa. 14:7)

Ideas

☐ *Photo journal.* Make a list of outdoor spaces. Take a walk through one, turning off your cell. Photograph whatever catches your eye.

☐ *Memory journal.* Write your fondest outdoor memories from the past (one-time moments or long-enjoyed rhythms). Were you riding a horse, swimming in a lake, running over grass, or stepping across a cool creek? How can you enjoy these outdoor spaces today?

☐ _____

5. **Choose Joy.** Investigate a new direction for joy, inspired by God's goodness, even if you're afraid.

Stand by the ways and see and ask for the ancient paths,
Where the good way is, and walk in it;
And you will find rest for your souls. (Jer. 6:16)

Ideas

☐ *Choose your "pink outfit."* Enjoy something that makes you happy. Pour oil and wine on the joy-wounded you. Delight in something just for you.

☐ *Follow Jesus downstream.* What can you investigate about yourself? How can you stop rowing upstream if you could say no? What would you say yes to?

☐ _____

Community

Enjoy a Friendship Mocha. A sweet treat of friendship is mixed in with soothing relational rest, dolloped with the whipped cream topping of an open heart.

6. **The Real You.** Seek out people with whom you can be your real self and laugh.

> Yes, brother, let me benefit from you in the Lord; refresh my heart in Christ. (Philem. 1:20)

Ideas

☐ *Ask an old friend* you haven't seen in a while out for coffee.

☐ *Make one new friendship* with someone you don't have to be or do anything special for—who shares a common interest, similar sense of humor, or comparable life challenges.

☐ *Visit a new gathering of people* as your "real self." Show up as you are: tired, even if you're just quiet with few words. Start online or in real life.

☐ _____

7. **In-the-Skin 1-on-1.** Get together with a friend 1-on-1 and share the deep things happening in your life. Choose to risk open-heart vulnerability over safety.

> I have come to have much joy and comfort in your love, because the hearts of the saints have been refreshed through you. (v. 7)

Ideas

☐ *Go out* to dinner or enjoy pancakes and eggs with a friend.

☐ *Share a "whitespace" story* that has surfaced as you've read this book. Share what's hard and what's good.

☐ *Tell her* you'd like hear her story. Simply listen.

☐ _____

⌁

Soul-Care

Enjoy a Soul-Care Espresso. A rejuvenating, freshly ground espresso shot of intimate rest, hand-pulled by the heart of Jesus, just for you.

8. **Body Rest.** Signal your body to physically rest knowing Jesus will carry you through. Sleep is a soul journey, not a turnkey solution.

> He enters into peace;
> They rest in their beds,
> Each one who walked in his upright way. (Isa. 57:2)

Ideas

Add whitespace cushion in your schedule through:

☐ *Touch.* Sitting in a light breeze, bathing, going to the spa, getting a massage, reading while snuggled in a fuzzy throw . . .

_____

☐ *Sound.* Playing ambient music, enjoying cyber stillness evenings, journaling *al fresco* in nature's surround-sound . . .

_____

☐ *Taste.* Slow eating, cooking fresh, slicing a fresh avocado into your sandwich, sipping a warm beverage . . .

_____

☐ *Scent.* Enjoy calming aromas like mint tea, grapefruit scented bath gel, and fresh flowers; baking from scratch; chopping fresh herbs . . .

☐ *Sight.* Enjoy a "better view" during your day—a splash of color, more sunlight, less stuff, more nature, more organization, more art . . .

☐ *Journaling.* Name your stress, freeing your thoughts unguarded.

☐ *Movement.* Light exercise, enjoying sunlight . . .

☐ *Single-tasking.*

---

9. **Heart Rest.** Spend time with Jesus. Rest is a gift we receive by bringing all parts of ourselves to him.

> Come to Me, all who are weary and heavy-laden, and I will give you rest. (Matt. 11:28)

Ideas

Receive *shalom* by recovering pieces of yourself:

☐ *Rest your story.* Write a letter to Jesus about the chapter you're living today.

☐ *Heal your past.* Write a letter to your younger self.

☐ *Let down your nets.* What dreams have you left behind? How is Jesus calling you to pick them up again?

☐ *Investigate your story.* Write down your *whys*, visit your childhood places, be curious by . . .

---

10. **Quiet Rest.** Enjoy intimately connecting with Jesus. Let go of the weight of guilt or the stress of *what's next.*

> Only in returning to me and resting in me will you be saved. In quietness and confidence is your strength. (Isa. 30:15 NLT 1996)

Ideas

Pray in quietness by:

☐ *Collecting God's love notes.* What reminds you God is thinking of you? Is it visual, emotional, tactile, experiential, social, intellectual, or practical?

☐ *Savoring one word from God.* What is one word surfacing in your heart? Where and when were you prompted: through Scripture, reading a book, watching a show, talking with a friend?

☐ *Movie-making with Jesus.* Pick a passage from the Gospels. Imagine stepping into the scene. What's capturing your attention: something happening or being said? How does it make you feel?

☐ *Journaling God's prayers for you.* Write a letter you imagine Jesus writing to you.

☐ *Listening/playing music.* What song or lyric touches you?

☐ *Walking/sitting outdoors,* enjoying a view with God.

☐ *Taking photographs* in silence and solitude.

☐ *Writing a letter to God.*

☐ _____

Engage Your Heart

As you browse this Whitespace Menu, which drink of soul rest are you most craving today?

Pick one or two drinks of soul rest you've brainstormed and let's head to the next chapter with drinks in hand—to explore the *how* of the Whitespace Challenge. As we do, resist the urge to view each idea as a to-do. Rest isn't a goal to achieve in thirty days.

Rest is a movement of faith—to engage your heart in a relationship. In intimacy. With Jesus.

Pull Up a Chair—Share

What one or two drinks on the Whitespace Menu are you most drawn to?

A Whitespace Prompt—Try This

Savor. Reflect on the word *savor* as you peruse the Whitespace Menu. Be sure to pick a *specific* whitespace drink before moving on with me to the next chapter. Don't think about it too much. There is no right one. It's like coffee tasting. We're whitespace sipping.

A Soul Conversation—Confide in Him

How does it feel to explore the different whitespace drinks? Is it sparking interest, or is it overwhelming? Share your thoughts with Jesus. He is curious about what you think.

25

serving it up

How

Now that you've brainstormed the *what*, let's talk about the *how*.

When you walk into a coffeehouse, you'll notice there's always a different coffee selection of the day. It's brewed fresh. Depending on your mood, a certain blend will taste especially yummy.

If you step up to an espresso bar, you can order an intense shot of java served in a gazillion different ways. One cup of joe at a café holds a change of scenery and time away. Each time the experience is different, because each drink is handcrafted.

Not only that, the coffee roasts also vary, depending on where they are sourced.

Coffee beans picked under different seasons—whether it's especially wet or dry—taste different. That's why *coffee blends* are created. Different blends are mixed to achieve a certain consistency in flavor.

In life, we go through dry seasons as well as wet ones, through no fault of our own. It's the weather of life. That's why the rest we need varies and the types of whitespace we blend and serve ourselves change season to season.

The texture of a coffee drink also depends on the roast. Some prefer the brightness of a lighter roast, while others want a smokier, heavier roast. Sometimes we just want decaf. Or maybe you pass on coffee altogether, opting for chai instead.

Taking in a sip of whitespace is the same. Sometimes resting in whitespace is light and bright. Other times it is intense and deep.

The point is this: your cup of whitespace rest—like your coffee—is uniquely customized for you.

Where?

One whitespace prompt for *location* can be your feelings. Where do you like to go if you're feeling lonely or happy?

Mood can be another prompt. What places put you in a creative, meditative, or active space?

A developing interest—no matter how slight—can trigger ideas on places to explore. Where can you connect with your passion?

The child in you also provides wonderful prompts: your memories and dreams. Where did you once love to go or wish you could have gone? Visit new places you wouldn't ordinarily go.

Be curious.

How Long? How Often?

The duration and frequency of whitespace is going to vary. The amount you are craving or need will depend on the season you're in.

There is no one-size-fits-all.

Sometimes, all is you need is a short drip. *But there are days you need a double shot of rest.* You want a venti. You need more than an hour.

Maybe you prefer a small drink of whitespace more often, or maybe big, warm Adventure Lattes spaced further apart will be just the thing. Sometimes all you can steal away might be two hours in the morning, once a month.

When Josh and Caleb were preschoolers, my whitespace was a monthly Creative Cappuccino—combined with sips of Soul-Care Espressos tucked in between. I'll sip God's love notes in a song, a hot bath, a few chapters of a book, entries in a journal, along with a Friendship Mocha here or there. That one monthly Creative Cappuccino morning felt like a glorious gazillion light-years. As the boys get older, I hope to sample some new Adventure Lattes.

When?

When you choose your whitespace moments is also fluid. Free yourself to sample different days and times. Don't force yourself into a rhythm.

Let the *what* and *where* of whitespace influence your pick of time or day. What day or time best allows you to enjoy your place or mode of resting?

As you sample different whitespaces, you'll naturally find what you crave and when best to feed your soul. You will find your rhythm. You will slowly, over time, develop an ambition to rest, fueled by the Holy Spirit prompting your soul rather than by guilt.

The important thing is to give yourself permission—to find your spiritual whitespace. As you start feeding your soul, you'll naturally get creative in finding a variety of ways to get your cup of rest.

The Invitation:
Whitespace Challenge

Now, you are ready to take the Whitespace Challenge with me. (Yes, you are!) I'm inviting you to enjoy a cup of spiritual whitespace sometime this month.

The Whitespace Challenge

The Purpose

To awaken your soul and enjoy resting with God, as you are.

The Details

1. Do something that encourages you to *feed your soul*, avoiding activities that are performance-oriented or focused on meeting expectations.
2. Choose an activity that carries an element of *quietness*.
3. *Enjoy* it with a cup of coffee or a brew of tea (encouraged, but not required).

Each person's whitespace looks different. How do *you* create whitespace?

Serve It Up and Schedule It

It's time to mark whitespace on your calendar (yes!).

Look back at the Whitespace Menu you brainstormed in the previous chapter. Which two whitespace drinks generated the most interest (scribbles)? Feel free to pick two of the same drink (i.e., two Creative Cappuccinos).

What did you choose? Is it a new recipe to cook for slow eating or a set of sheer sky-blue curtains to try hanging for a soulful home? Pick a day on the calendar to say no to anything that prevents your

Adventure Latte. This is your soul time with God, to permeate a delicious aroma or spark color in your home.

Or are you driving to the art store to pick up brush and paint—or is it to Target you're heading, to grab some tea, a ballpoint pen, and a journal? Write it down on your shopping list. Enjoy a Creative Cappuccino.

Maybe schedule a Saturday morning to enjoy a Soul-Care Espresso on a dusty trail or at the beach—or grab a Friendship Mocha at a café.

Remember, don't pressure yourself into making this a regularly occurring event on your calendar. Mark it on the calendar for this one time only.

Breathe in whitespace free of commitment. You can order another whitespace drink later. Enjoy this one for now.

Your Whitespace Drink Order

Ready to place your order? Okay. It's time to write down your spiritual whitespace drink order.

Whitespace Drink #1

(check one) ☐ Creative Cappuccino
☐ Friendship Mocha
☐ Adventure Latte
☐ Soul-Care Espresso

What: (e.g., Soul-Care Espresso: take a walk and journal a letter to Jesus near the creek.)

_____

Where: (Rancho San Antonio Trail. Close by.)

_____

When: (Early Saturday morning when kids and hubby are still fresh. Be back midmorning, before lunch.)

Date/Time: (8/17, 8:30–10:30 a.m.)

Whitespace Step: (Ask hubby if he can hang out with kids that morning.)

Whitespace Drink #2

(check one) ☐ Creative Cappuccino
             ☐ Friendship Mocha
             ☐ Adventure Latte
             ☐ Soul-Care Espresso

What: (e.g., Creative Cappuccino: bedtime bath reading.)

Where: (Bathtub.)

When: (After kids are down and no more curtain calls.)

Date/Time: (Anytime I can do it this week, 9 p.m.)

Whitespace Step: (Buy my favorite bath gel. I don't want to use the babywash anymore. Find that new book—where did I put it?)

Coffee gives us glimpses into the complexity and sensitivity our tongue has to flavor and texture. Can you imagine how far greater and unique is the palate of the soul God created in you?

What tastes sweet or smells fragrant to us is shaped by our personal set of experiences. God sees the *innermost you*—and it is his heart's desire to awaken your soul, so you can rest with him today.

Your drinks are all lined up now. Ready? What's holding you back? In the next chapter, I'll share my top eight whitespace killers and triggers.

Pull Up a Chair—Share

How did it feel to write down your *spiritual whitespace drink order*?

What was easy or hard about it?

A Whitespace Prompt—Try This

Make it real. Be sure to brainstorm a "whitespace step" with your drink order. *Tell someone* about how your whitespace experiment went. Be careful to share your experience with a whitespace friend (someone who supports or shares your desire for soulful rest).

A Soul Conversation—Confide in Him

It's natural to feel resistant or hear questions pop up in your mind about how this would really work out. Just give voice to your doubts or concerns. This is hard stuff—the feeding of your soul—but your soul oh-so-wants it.

26

whitespace killers
and triggers

When my husband asked me out on our first date, it wasn't what I expected. I had daydreamed about it for weeks. A romantic night out in the city? Maybe tickets to a play or concert?

Nope. He wanted to take me to the movies. In the afternoon. I was used to going out at night. We finished dinner before nine o'clock.

As I slipped into the passenger seat of his blue Camaro while Eric held the door, I thought *maybe he's taking me out for a stroll somewhere.*

Nope. He said he had a great time and began to steer the conversation in the same direction our car was driving. Home. It was goodnight.

Standing in the elevator going up to my third-floor apartment, I had to confront the possibility. *Maybe he doesn't like me as much as I like him.* This was the conclusion I drew, based on stipulations I had put on what constituted a "romantic" evening.

We often do the same thing when it comes to enjoying spiritual whitespace—spending 1-on-1 time with God. We make up rules on time well spent.

Let's rewrite some of those rules.

This is where *whitespace killers* and *whitespace triggers* come in. Whitespace killers hold us back, while whitespace triggers help us rest. Let's first expose the whitespace killers. Here are my top eight.

Top Eight Whitespace Killers

1. **Time Minimum.** I must spend x minutes with God in order for it to count.
2. **Procrastination Disqualifier.** If I've procrastinated x number of hours (or days or weeks), God is disappointed. I'm in the whitespace doghouse.
3. **White Glove Test.** My house (or fill in the blank) needs to be cleaner and neater. How can I get spiritually in tune with God when my room is (or when I am) a mess?
4. **Goal-oriented Perfectionism.** I must stick with "the plan" to prove my devotion to God (fill in whatever spiritual "fitness" program to complete in x timeframe).
5. **Nostalgia.** I've always done whitespace "this way." Tailoring time with God to meet my current set of needs or preferences would not be spiritual.
6. **Guilt.** My friends/husband/children/family will feel left out. They'll feel hurt and think I want to get away from them. I feel selfish.
7. **Superwoman Syndrome.** The world would crash if I stopped. My husband is too burnt-out himself. I don't want to burden anyone.
8. **Waste of Time.** There's not enough time as it as. Focusing on myself is childish, impractical, or wrong.

When we put rules on how God can connect with us, we stop feeding our souls—during the times we need it most. We miss enjoying the most amazing architecture God designed in us. Our soul.

It's part of God's greatest commandment. To love him with all our soul.[1]

Architectural Atmosphere

In architectural and spatial design, there is a term used called "architectural atmosphere." Architects argue that space is designed and built for people *to use and experience.* We can only sense the atmosphere of a space by inhabiting it ourselves.

Simply looking at photographs or reading about other people's experiences can never replace our experience of using a space personally.

Atmosphere is created when we bring our memories, thoughts, and emotions to a place. *It is our physical presence that makes a space become real.*

In the same way, there is a quality of life—an architectural atmosphere—we can only experience *if we awaken our souls and use it to rest.* German philosopher Gernot Böhme writes about architectural atmosphere, saying "we must be physically present" to experience space in its complete entirety.[2]

This principle applies to taking time out for spiritual whitespace. Feeding your soul is one way to physically *be present* with God and interact with him.[3] We are using what God created—our body (touch, taste, smell, sight, and hearing), our sensitivities (what we like and don't like), our emotions (positive and negative), and our artistic interests—to enjoy his presence in us.

> Do you not know that you are a temple of God and that the Spirit of God dwells in you? (1 Cor. 3:16)

Just as there are architectural elements—light, sound, materials, breathing space, furniture, and other objects—that help us experience the atmosphere of a building, there are *whitespace triggers* that help awaken our soul to rest.

Eight Whitespace Triggers

Here are eight whitespace triggers that have helped me rest during my year of post-traumatic stress disorder.

1. Small Is Big

When you've hit a dry spell, whitespace comes in brief glimpses, like fog lifting in patches, only to disappear quickly. Take any opportunity as it presents itself to enjoy quiet or slow during your day, even if it's whisper-thin.

Jesus sees those slivers of whitespace we spend as two small copper coins—big in God's heart—just like the ones a poor widow placed into the temple offering.[4] Jesus sees the weight of your faith. The smallest movements bring God the greatest pleasure.

2. Do the Opposite

When you get an idea to rest, don't be surprised to hear yourself come up with endless reasons why your idea is no good. Whose voice is that really? This is how you've always protected yourself, by cutting out pleasure and rest.

Do the opposite. Follow your heart's prompting. Do what you fear.

Behind that fear lies your true self, whom Jesus loves and accepts unconditionally. Surely the blind man who heard Jesus spit on the ground and felt something wet and gooey on his eyelids must have felt intimidated walking through a crowded city to wash himself in a pool. Yet that is how Jesus restored him.

3. That's Right, I Don't Deserve It

Because you've been "bad"—you've just yelled at your kids, you were grumpy with your spouse, or you messed up x or y again—you may punish yourself by withholding something good for your soul.

Don't believe this. Times like these are when you *most need the rest* and comfort of your heavenly Father.

You can tell yourself: *That's right, I don't deserve it. But God will give me what I need. I can receive grace—as is.*[5]

You'll return from whitespace a little more loved, softened by a deeper rest, to love others as is too.

4. Swap Whitespace

At first, my kids didn't like Mom heading out somewhere "fun" without them. I explained whitespace was like Mommy going out for a haircut. I'm taking care of me. I assure them I'll do something fun with them later in the week (special board game time together, an ice-cream outing, etc.).

This models the message that spending time with God isn't a chore but something pleasurable and important.

What whitespace would your kids enjoy with you? *Swap a whitespace time by doing something soul-feeding with them.* They'll love it.

When I first introduced the idea to my husband, I confessed to him I felt guilty for asking. But I assured Eric I would help *him* get a break for whitespace on the calendar too. Acknowledge the stress your spouse is under. Express your support to give him time to enjoy a hobby, time outdoors, or friendship with Jesus. Appreciate his willingness to try it once. Then negotiate calendar dates/times so *each of you* can enjoy whitespace without guilt.

Start small.

Another way to swap whitespace is with other moms. This might be a once-in-a-while thing, but it opens up great conversations about stress in general.

5. Cyber Stillness—Leave Room for Cream

Rather than viewing technology as bad, simply leave "room for cream" in your schedule.

Choose *cyber stillness* during your whitespace. Turn off your phone. Put your computer to sleep. Fill that space with beauty and rest.

6. Whitespace Friends

Challenge yourself to find—and slowly develop—Whitespace Friends: friends who can support or share in your journey of soulful rest.

OPEN-HEART IRL FRIENDS

Someone in-real-life (IRL) you can go deep with. Who values vulnerability. Who can see you—and you can see her—*unedited*, when you're sick with worry, giddy with excitement, or plain old beige and in-between (e.g., take a walk together, invite yourself over, go out for coffee).

SOULFUL-INTEREST FRIENDS

Someone on a similar whitespace journey to explore a similar passion or interest, to share ideas, discoveries, struggles, and challenges.

This can be IRL or online (blogging together, photography, art, dance, sports, music, reading, etc.).

Which one comes first is unique to your personality. These two types of friendships ignite each other. Maybe for you, they are one and the same.

Me? I found my first *soulful-interest friends* online when I put out the Whitespace Challenge on my blog. As readers and I swapped stories, I felt so much less alone. Putting things in writing helped me verbalize what was happening inside.

It made me hunger for and seek out more restful relationships—in real life. Just one or two *open-heart IRL friends* was the perfect number for me.

7. *Tea, Music, and New Wineskins*

Don't underestimate the power of *soul prompts* to get you into a restful mood. Prepare something aromatic like steeping tea or body-soothing like drawing a hot bath. Music also opens your heart without one word spoken. Lyrics have become our modern-day poetry.

Give yourself permission to find new wineskins to rest.[6]

8. *Whitespace Retreats*

Take whitespace on the road. Sometimes I take half-day trips to the ocean. Once a year, I find a Christian retreat somewhere and use the "free time" to read and journal with God. One special type of whitespace retreat I enjoy is finding One Word from God for the new year. What would you like to do with God for an extended period of time?

Taste the Atmosphere

After that first date I was so worried whether my hubby-to-be was attracted and really enjoying time with me—I focused on the wrong indicators.

I discounted how we had lost track of time and how our cheeks ached from all the laughing. We had talked as old friends reunited, filling in pieces the other missed throughout the years. We could sit and be quiet. Sip our coffee without pressure to fill the space.

Conversation. That's why Eric planned the theater for the afternoon, not the evening. He wanted to grab a cup of coffee together beforehand, to get to know me.

Considerate. Eric set up an earlier dinner so we could enjoy each other's company without the pressure to have it go late into the night (if *I* wasn't into him).

Gracious. He didn't want to be pushy for more time after dinner. He was afraid I'd say yes because I was too polite to say no.

So you see, I got the signals all wrong. Eric didn't just tolerate spending time with me. He was falling in love. And so was I.

Taking time out to enjoy spiritual whitespace is an intimate movement of faith.

Dare to awaken your soul to be physically present.

Taste the atmosphere with God and bring all the stories you're living—the joy, heartbreak, worries, hopes, and dreams that lie deep within—and find your home with Jesus.

Our journey to rest, after all, is a homecoming to become the beloved.

To rest. As is.

Pull Up a Chair—Share

What are your biggest *whitespace killers?*

What are your *whitespace triggers?*

A Whitespace Prompt—Try This

Be encouraged. This is a journey we all have in common. See if you can find likeminded friends to talk about the whitespace killers that cross your path and swap whitespace triggers that can help you rest.

A Soul Conversation—Confide in Him

How can you be more present with God both physically and emotionally?

afterword

I'm standing at the edge of town.

This isn't a city you can see on a map. But I have been living in this place for a very long time. *This city is called survival.* I have been a city builder, creating makeshift shelters of safety. But my city has crumbled.

Where do I go now? I ask Jesus.

Look beside you, Jesus answers. *Who is holding your hand?*

It's Jesus. He is calling me to journey to a new city not made with hands. It dawns on me, as my heart pulses through my fingertips. *I want to go back. To fixing and building again.*

But Jesus points me ahead. He wants to awaken my soul with *his presence.* He wants me to rest.

What do you do with a story that goes off script? I'm leaving mine as is. I'm living my story with whitespaces. I'm walking into the desert, trusting there will be roadways and rivers. I've seen the devastation but I haven't been abandoned.

I don't have to wait until I'm unafraid. I don't have to be sure and I don't need to know the way. I have what I need for this journey.

I've found the little girl lost and I'm not letting go. We both have Jesus now.

I am leaving my city of stress. I don't have to go back. A new story is coming alive.

I'm learning to live it in my everyday life. New. As is.

Between the Pages

I may not have met you, but I'm trusting that somehow you've found pieces of your faith story as you've heard mine. You are hearing your soul speak and you are catching echoes of Jesus whispering back to you.

If you and I could walk down an old dirt road, to find a big oak tree, to sit and lean against it on either side, I'd listen to your whitespace stories. I'd love hearing what resting in whitespace might look like for you. How would you make room for whitespace?

You know, friend, God put us here between the pages of this book to keep each other company. I've wondered if there was someone like you, who would understand this travel of faith and rest.

Now that you're here, journey with me. Gather your stories, the ones you're living—as well as the ones you've uncovered in each chapter—the ones that are written on your heart with ink that can't be seen.

A Blank Space

Because Jesus is taking us on a journey to awaken our souls, this book is only a beginning—that starts over again each and every day.

Life is a story. Every line begins with blank space. Every chapter a new page.

It's not easy. To know just what to do.

Looking into the whitespace, it's tempting to turn back and do life as we've always done it. But the story God is writing in us wants to break through. It's *your heart* he wants to touch, *your hand* he takes in his, and *your face* into which he longs to gaze.

He wants to bring you close into his embrace, to hear him whisper your name. So you can journey ahead and find rest for your soul. Just as you are. With Jesus and others.

Awaken Your Soul

Rest is a journey we weren't meant to make alone. We need each other.

Rest may not come instantaneously, but slowly sweetens, the way honey drips into tea. It comes tenderly, the way a woman tastes her first kiss with the man who will promise a lifetime of being hers. It settles gently, the way yellow melts into a pale evening sky.

Come and journey.

Find the spiritual whitespaces in your everyday life and in your story with me.

Let's keep each other company. Life can be beautiful, even if it isn't easy, because God has a whitespace story in you.

It's a shot of faith. Hearing God's story echoing in you. It's soul comforting, isn't it? When we know we are not alone. Together, we can find moments of refuge, where our friendship allows us to travel together.

Take the challenge to find your spiritual whitespace with Jesus. Awaken your soul to rest.

Discover the many ways God whispers to us, *You belong to me.*

Give your soul the rest it longs for and bring all of yourself to be present. We can learn to take care of that little girl.

So she can tell his story by living it, as it's made in us. Today. Together. Let's make room for spiritual whitespace.

You are a letter of Christ . . . written not with ink but with the Spirit of the living God, not on tablets of stone but on tablets of human hearts. (2 Cor. 3:3)

a note from the author

Dear Friend,

I feel so grateful to have someone to share my journey with. Thank you for being a part of my story. This book has come to a close but the words we've shared between these pages don't have to end. There is a community of faith friends I've found online at my blog FaithBarista.com and I'd like to share them with you on this journey of rest.

We've swapped stories together. They've encouraged me so much.

Now I'd like to invite you to join us too.

If you've enjoyed expressing your heart through journaling in this book, continue to explore your faith journey with me. Every week I serve up whitespace prompts—to trigger ideas, inspire soul conversations, and awaken our souls to experience rest.

If you like to write, share your voice with us in community.

If reading feeds your soul, simply be present by enjoying the encouraging quotes, tools, and resources I'll be sharing, to keep you company on your journey.

And my favorite part of all: I would love to exchange ideas on how to feed our souls, ways to take care of the lives God has given us, and enjoy whitespace in deeper measure.

Let's encourage each other. We are not alone. I look forward to meeting you.

Your story is important. Your voice is beautiful—God in you. As is.

With appreciation,

Bonnie

FaithBarista.com
Facebook.com/TheBonnieGray
Twitter.com/TheBonnieGray
TheBonnieGray.com

acknowledgments

If I knew ten years ago I'd experience PTSD, I would have never said yes when Eric proposed. I would have rather suffered alone than have someone as beautiful and deserving of happiness as my husband suffer alongside me.

Thank you, Eric, for allowing your heart to break with mine. Thank you for sacrificing your emotional and physical reserves—to take care of me and the boys—so I could heal, find my voice, and write this book. I'm forever grateful for you. I love you.

Thank you to Chip MacGregor, my agent, for going the distance with me on this literary journey and doing so with such expertise, commitment, and kindness.

Thank you to the people at Revell, who stood by me to release this story to print. Thank you to Twila Bennett, Michele Misiak, and Robin Barnett for launching this book and to the sales teams for building relationships so it can be read.

I am especially grateful to Vicki Crumpton, my editor. Thank you for having faith in the journey of a living manuscript. The amazing editing work you do is spiritual work, bringing healing, clarifying the unsaid.

None of this could have been possible without confidantes who journeyed with me in everyday life, carrying me with countless prayers and unwavering kindness—like friends lowering the paralytic to Jesus's healing presence. Thank you, Merrianne Young, Carol Lind, Holley Gerth, Annette Makarewycz, Elaine Herbert, Amy Joh, Sally Forster, Sayaka Tomine, and Naemi Strobel for loving me. Thank you, Pastor John Riemenschnitter, Doug Goins, Coach Ken Mburu, and The Highway Community for helping me embrace brokenness as a holy journey in community.

A special thanks belongs to friends who have journeyed with me since I first wrote in my broken voice: the readers at FaithBarista .com. Thank you for opening your heart and sharing your stories. I'm so grateful God led me to find my voice—with you. You gave me courage to make this book real.

I'd like to also thank Donald Miller for his book *A Million Miles in a Thousand Years*, which inspired me to live a better story, and also Steve Arterburn, whose book *Healing Is a Choice* freed me to investigate and seek out a therapist.

Thank you to the DaySpring team and (in)courage sisters for your support and encouragement, making writing in community a reality, not just a slogan.

Lastly, I want to thank Dr. P. There is no way on earth I could journey through such treacherous waters as childhood trauma on my own. Thank you for bringing a lifetime's worth of experience and the skill of guiding others like me through and out. Over and over again. I'm so grateful for the tremendous compassion and spiritual wisdom you employed helping the little girl in me to find Jesus and heal.

Finally, Jesus. Thank you for not leaving me. Thank you for walking the lonely and broken road long ago and walking it again with me today. Thank you for loving the little girl in me. Keep holding on to me. I need you. I love you.

notes

Chapter 1 Desolate Places

1. BibleStudyTools.com, *Eremos*, "The NAS New Testament Greek Lexicon," http://www.biblestudytools.com/lexicons/greek/nas/eremos.html.

Chapter 2 Wallpapered Memories

1. For an additional perspective on this story, one which really encouraged me in my healing process, I recommend Stephen Arterburn, *Healing Is a Choice* (Nashville: Thomas Nelson, 2005), xx–xxiv.

2. Ibid., 213–14.

Chapter 3 The Toy Store

1. Robert Rachenberg, *White Painting*, 1951, oil on canvas, MOMA, San Francisco.

Chapter 5 The Screen Door

1. Keith Robertson, "White Space," http://www.logoorange.com/white-space. php. Originally published in *Émigré* 26, 1993.

Chapter 6 The Basement

1. Brennan Manning and John Blase, *All Is Grace* (Colorado Springs: David C. Cook, 2011), 51.

2. See 2 Corinthians 3:12–18. Moses kept a veil over his face to hide fading glory. But we are free to live "unveiled" (our inadequate, authentic selves) because the Holy Spirit in us gives us "ever-increasing glory."

Chapter 8 Insomnia

1. See Mark 5:35–43.
2. See Mark 5:1–20.
3. See Joel 2:24–26.

Chapter 9 Clutter

1. See 1 Kings 17:7–16.

Chapter 10 The Bookcase

1. See John 6:27–66.

Chapter 12 The Phone Call

1. See Matthew 10:14.

Chapter 14 The Hallway

1. For more information on this concept, see Holley Gerth, *You're Made for a God-Sized Dream* (Grand Rapids: Revell, 2013).

Chapter 17 Solitude

1. Robert MacNeil, Arthur Rubenstein, "Arthur Rubenstein at 90," Great Performances television series, season 5, episode 9, January 26, 1977 (West Germany: Unitel).
2. As quoted in Susan Cain, "The Rise of the New Groupthink," *New York Times*, January 13, 2012, http://www.nytimes.com/2012/01/15/opinion/sunday/the-rise-of-the-new-groupthink.html?pagewanted=all&_r=0.
3. See Revelation 8:4.
4. See 2 Corinthians 6:16.

Chapter 18 The Wild Things

1. See Exodus 3:1–4.

Chapter 23 A New Ambition

1. Matthew May, "Break Through by Taking Breaks," *Open Forum*, September 17, 2009, https://www.openforum.com/articles/break-through-by-taking-breaks-1/.
2. Ibid.
3. Ibid.
4. The Greek word for "ambition" is *philotimeomai*, used in Romans 15:20, 2 Corinthians 5:9, and 1 Thessalonians 4:11. See http://www.biblestudytools.com/lexicons/greek/nas/philotimeomai.html.

Chapter 24 A Menu

1. Matthew May, "The Art of Whitespace," *Blogging Innovation*, September 17, 2009, http://www.business-strategy-innovation.com/2009/09/art-of-whitespace.html.

Chapter 26 Whitespace Killers and Triggers

1. See Luke 10:27.
2. Gernot Böhme, "Atmosphere as the Subject Matter of Architecture," in *Natural Histories* (Switzerland: Herzog and de Meuron, 2005), 402.
3. See Acts 17:26.
4. See Mark 12:41–44.
5. See Matthew 6:33; Hebrews 4:16.
6. Matthew 9:14–17.

Bonnie Gray is the soulful writer behind *Faith Barista*, serving up shots of faith for everyday life. She is a featured contributor for DaySpring (in)courage and her work is also nationally syndicated on Crosswalk.com. After graduating from UCLA, Bonnie served as a missionary, ministry entrepreneur, and Silicon Valley high-tech professional. She lives in Northern California with her husband, Eric, and their two sons, and blogs about her fascination with the challenge of keeping faith hot and fresh in the daily grind at www.faithbarista.com.

Connect with Bonnie
FaithBarista.com
Twitter.com/TheBonnieGray
Facebook.com/TheBonnieGray
TheBonnieGray.com

connect with
BONNIE
on her blog
Faith Barista

Find resources for
personal or group study.

faithbarista.com

TheBonnieGray | @TheBonnieGray